THE WILD

GUIDE TO

SEX

AND LOVING

THE WILD

GUIDE TO

SEX

AND LOVING

SIOBHAN KELLY

Ulysses Press

Published in the United States by
Ulysses Press
P.O. Box 3440
Berkeley, CA 94703
www.ulyssespress.com

10 9 8 7 6 5 4 3 2 1

First published in Great Britain in 2002 by Ebury Press
Random House, 20 Vauxhall Bridge Road, London SW1V 2SA

Library of Congress Control Number 2002110058
ISBN 1-56975-338-5

Edited by Rachel Aris
Art direction by Jack Buchan
Interior designed by Seagulls
Cover designed by Sarah Levin
Make-up by Bettina Graham
Photography by John Freeman, assisted by Alex Dow

Papers used are natural, recyclable products made from wood grown in
sustainable forests.

Printed and bound in Singapore

Distributed in the United States by Publishers Group West

Contents

foreword

Welcome to **The Wild Guide to Sex and Loving**.

Informative, fun and packed with new and exciting sex tips guaranteed to set your pulse racing, this book is designed to inspire you and your partner to relax with each other and explore your sensuality. For it's worth remembering that, whether you're just getting acquainted or have been together for years, there is always room for improvement!

The Wild Guide to Sex and Loving is as diverse as it is educational. Everything from foreplay to role play, and from Tantric sex to sex toys is explored, showing you how to enrich new relationships as well as revitalise old ones, while adding an extra twist to your bedroom antics.

Stimulation doesn't have to be solely physical: it can also be a state of mind. This book will fire your imaginations and make you aware of the endless possibilities there are for having fun in the bedroom. It is paramount that you both feel comfortable, so relax, read on, and open your eyes to the new, sexy and exciting directions your relationship can take!

Happy loving,

Jacqueline Gold
Chief Executive, Ann Summers

1

lips, hips and fingertips

his pleasure Zones

Men's bodies are incredibly sensitive and packed with far more erogenous zones than the obvious one that gets all the press (for a list of the most popular non-genital hotspots, see right)! Below you'll find a brief guided tour around every man's pride and joy – but for more on how to handle a naked man, turn to pages 42–44 and 52–54.

The penis

There's no such thing as a 'typical' penis – penises vary wildly in colour, shape and size from guy to guy. But they all have the same basic components…

The shaft This is the 'stalk' of the penis. A vessel called the urethra, which runs up the centre of the shaft, transports urine and semen through the penis. The skin here is very thin and sensitive, and is packed with nerve endings. The average penis is 6.5–10.5 cm long when flaccid, and 15–18 cm when erect. It's a myth that you can predict the size of a guy's manhood from the size of his nose, feet, hands or height – the only scientific method of determining the size of a man's penis is to take down his trousers and measure it!

Head The smooth, curved tip of the penis is also known as the glans and has an even higher concentration of nerve endings than the shaft, making it the most erogenous area of the male body. Semen and urine leave the body through the tiny opening at the tip of the head.

Foreskin The head of an uncircumcised penis is covered in a protective layer of loose skin called the foreskin, which wrinkles up when the penis is flaccid. When the penis is erect, the foreskin

His top 10 hotspots

1 Scalp and hairline
2 Neck and shoulders
3 Ear lobes and inner ear
4 Mouth and lips
5 Small of back
6 Chest and nipples
7 Arms and hands
8 Bum and anus
9 Legs and feet
10 Stomach

retracts to expose the glans and allow semen to pass through. It's thin, hairless and on the inside produces a natural mucus called smegma, which can take on a cheesy odour if the area under the foreskin isn't washed gently with warm water on a regular basis. Circumcision is the surgical removal of the foreskin, and is usually performed for religious or hygiene reasons – some say that a circumcised penis is cleaner and more sensitive.

Frenulum The foreskin is attached to the head of the penis by a tiny triangle of super-sensitive skin on the underside of the shaft called the frenulum. It's so sensitive that even the tiniest lick or nibble here can trip a man over the edge to orgasm.

Testicles Designed to manufacture sperm and the male sex hormone testosterone, the testicles hang loosely behind the penis in a little sack of skin called the scrotum. It's normal for one testicle to hang lower than the other, so that they don't chafe when their owner walks and runs. The line that runs down the scrotum between the balls, known as the raphe, is another highly erogenous zone.

The prostate gland This gland, which makes prostatic fluid (one of the ingredients of semen), is located a couple of centimetres or so up the front wall of the rectum. Often referred to as the male G-spot, it's incredibly sensitive to pressure. Men who enjoy receiving anal sex report that stimulation of the prostate gland can enhance orgasm.

Perineum This hairless patch of skin between his balls and his anus is incredibly sensitive to stimulation because of its high concentration of nerve endings and its proximity to the prostate gland.

The male sexual response

Men experience four different levels of arousal. Although most of the sensations of orgasm are concentrated in a man's penis and the pelvis area, a climax affects the muscle tension and blood flow in his entire body.

Phase one, excitement: 'Mmm, that's nice'

When a man is exposed to sexually arousing stimuli, there's a sudden increase in the blood flow to his penis and scrotum. The penis becomes engorged with blood and stands erect. As it does so, it changes colour as well as size and shape: it darkens and large blue veins stand out on the surface. At the same time, his adrenal glands release the hormone adrenaline, which causes his heart rate, blood pressure and breathing rate to rise.

Phase two, plateau: 'Ooooooh'

He gets a full erection and might leak a little semen from the end of his penis. The testicles can increase in size by up to 50 per cent, and they're pulled against the body wall. The sperm gathers and gets propelled up the urethra: once it's there, ready to be shot, he's reached the point of no return, known as 'ejaculatory inevitability' – orgasm is on the way and he's coming, ready or not, even if stimulation stops. This lasts about 3 seconds and then...

Phase three, orgasm: 'Yes! Yes! Yes!'

Ejaculation occurs when the ring of muscle or sphincter at the tip of the penis opens like a floodgate and lets the semen shoot out. The male orgasm consists of about 5 muscle contractions, 0.8 seconds apart, generally lasting between 4 and 11 seconds. The longer it's been since he's had sex, the more semen he'll produce. A lot of men shout or grimace as they come, or their body takes over and they jerk their pelvis, pushing it in as far as it'll go.

About a teaspoon of semen is pumped out during orgasm.

Phase four, resolution: 'Aaaaah'

In the first few seconds after orgasm, the penis, particularly the head, will be incredibly sensitive to touch and may even feel painful. It only takes a minute or so for the penis and testicles to start decreasing in size, however, and they usually return to their pre-aroused state within about 10 minutes. In the hours that follow, the penis will be relatively insensitive to stimulation and erection will be quite hard to achieve. As a rule, the younger a man is, the sooner he'll be ready to go again!

her pleasure Zones

Women are more dependent than men on all-over body stimulation and skin-on-skin contact for sexual arousal. It's also worth noting that women say *how* you touch them is just as important as *where* you touch them. For detailed information on her favourite non-genital hotspots, see overleaf.

What's up down there? A guide to female genitalia

There are as many variations on the theme of female genitalia as there are women, but this inch-by-inch guide will take you through the basics…

The clitoris Stroking and caressing the clitoris, also known as the magic button, is the most sure-fire way for most women to reach orgasm. Nowhere else in the human body – male or female – are there so many sensitive nerve endings packed into such a tight space. You can find the clitoris under a tiny hood of skin at the top of the vulva. The only visible part is the tip, which looks like a tiny pinkish bud – but the blood vessels and nerve endings attached to it go back as far as 5 cm.

Labia The word 'labia' is Latin for lips, and there are two sets that (together with the clitoris) make up the vulva, or the external genitalia. The labia majora, or outer lips, are fleshy folds of skin, hairy on the outside and with sweat glands on the inside. They vary wildly in shape, size and colour from woman to woman, depending on age and ethnic group. During the reproductive years they're full and fleshy. Just inside these are the labia minora – hairless folds of skin that extend from the front of the vulva, where the clitoral hood is found, right to the back. They secrete hormones that make the genitals smell sexually attractive. In some women the labia minora are tucked inside the labia majora, while in others the inner lips protrude beyond the outer ones.

Hymen This refers to the thin membrane of skin that covers the opening of the vagina – long gone in most adult women. Historically, an intact hymen was used to prove virginity but it can in fact be broken by non-sexual activities such as horse riding and inserting a tampon. Unbroken, it has a tiny opening to let vaginal secretions and menstrual blood through, and can bleed when it's ruptured.

Perineum This tiny, hairless patch of skin between her vagina and anus is sensitive to stimulation despite being so tough.

Vagina This long elastic muscular tube is the hostess for the penis during intercourse. It's an average of 9 cm in length in its resting state, but can stretch sufficiently to form the birth canal for a baby, so it is more than flexible enough to accommodate any penis. The vaginal wall is made up of rings of tough, stretchy muscle. During sexual arousal, the vagina swells with blood and produces mucus-like lubrication. The bottom third of the vagina is the most sensitive to stimulation: sensation dulls the further up the vagina you go.

The G-spot Named after Dr Ernst Grafenburg, the German gynaecologist who first identified it, the G-spot is a highly erogenous zone located about 5 cm up on the front wall of the vagina. This mass of nerve tissue can't be felt unless it's stimulated, whether that's by a finger, a penis or a sex toy, and is said to be the size of a small baked bean. It's highly controversial – lots of women say that stimulation on the front of the vaginal wall does nothing for them, and that the G-spot doesn't exist. Others swear that it does and have the orgasms to prove it.

Cervix Found at the point where the vagina meets the uterus, the cervix is round and firm with a tiny dimple the size of a pinhead where menstrual blood (and babies) leave the body. Some women are sensitive to stimulation here.

Her top 10 hotspots
1 Back of neck and ear lobes
2 Shoulders
3 Face, scalp and hairline
4 Breasts and nipples
5 Mouth
6 Arms, armpits and hands
7 Legs and feet, especially inner thighs and backs of knees
8 Bottom
9 Stomach
10 Back

A sex workout

Improve intercourse with this once-a-day muscle-toning exercise. The pubococcygeal muscle, also known as the PC muscle, is located in your pelvis and links your genitals to the rest of your pelvic floor (your genitals, your perineum and your sphincters). Toning it can change your sex life forever — and you don't need to go to a gym to do so. All the equipment you need is already in your underwear!

Find your PC muscle the next time you go to the toilet: both men and women use this muscle to stop and start the flow of urine. When you contract the muscle you should feel your whole pelvic floor tensing up.

The exercise couldn't be easier: simply contract the PC muscle for a few seconds, relax for a few seconds and repeat. Begin with 15 contractions of 10 seconds each, and work up to 50 a day. You'll feel the difference within a fortnight to a month. No-one will know you're doing them, so there's no excuse not to make them part of your daily routine — in the queue for a train ticket, at your desk, while you're driving to work, walking round the supermarket. It's your sexy secret!

The benefits for men include increased sensitivity, the ability to sustain an erection for longer and greater control over when they ejaculate. Benefits for women include a well-toned vagina, which means you'll be able to grip and massage his penis much better during sex — as well as feeling tighter. These exercises are particularly good for women who feel they've lost some elasticity in the vaginal wall after having a baby and for more mature women who can't control the flow of urine as well as they once could. Because this is the muscle that spasms during female orgasm, toning it also makes for better, stronger and more frequent climaxes.

Having found this muscle and established control over it, women should try flexing it during intercourse. If you can sense he's about to come, squeeze hard and make his orgasm unforgettable! A word of warning though: crush him with your love muscle in the few seconds after his orgasm and he'll wince with pain — the head of his penis is too sensitive to handle all that stimulation while he's recovering from his climax.

The big 'O'

So what actually happens to our bodies in those few fabulous seconds that all the fuss is about? Men and women experience the same four basic stages of sexual arousal — excitement, plateau, orgasm and resolution — but they do so in different ways, and on a slightly different timescale.

Phase one, excitement: 'Mmm, that's nice'

During the excitement phase, blood rushes to the clitoris and vagina, swelling them and making them more sensitive to the touch. The breasts and lips also swell with blood, which makes them enlarge slightly, and the nipples become erect, bigger and darker. Many women report a throbbing sensation between the legs as well. Blood pressure and heart rate rise. These are the early stages of arousal – if you don't receive any stimulation, whether through kissing, caressing or direct genital contact, you'll easily return to your relaxed state.

Phase two, plateau: 'Ooooooh'

If you keep receiving stimulation, you'll enter the plateau phase. This sees yet more blood flowing to the genitals, and the lower third of the vagina narrows, getting ready to grip the penis. The rest of the vagina actually gets bigger, waiting for the sperm to be deposited. The uterus rises up to make room for the penis in a process called 'tenting'; there's evidence that stimulating the clitoris can cause this. Your vestibular glands, a couple of centimetres inside the vaginal wall, will start to produce lubrication in anticipation of penetration.

Phase three, orgasm: 'Yes! Yes! Yes!'

The moment you've been waiting for is an intense reflex that's concentrated in the genitals but has repercussions all over the body. It lasts no longer than 10–15 seconds, and consists of a series of rapid contractions, about 0.8 seconds apart, in the lower third of the vagina, which get less frequent as they go on. The muscles round your bladder and perineum contract too. You can have 5–15 of these contractions, depending on how intense your orgasm is. The clitoris retreats back under its hood and, as soon as orgasm is over, becomes incredibly sensitive – it might even feel painful to touch. The area around the nipple may contract and a dark flush, like a heat rash, can appear across the chest and breasts. Some women stay almost completely still and shudder in silence, others gasp or contort their faces as if in pain, and others still – you know who you are – shriek loudly enough to wake the dead.

Phase four, resolution: 'Aaaaah'

The flush across the breasts subsides, heart rate and breathing return to normal and, after 15 to 30 minutes, your genitals have returned to their pre-aroused state. The endorphins released into the bloodstream will have heightened your emotions – many women report feeling euphoric, vulnerable, energised or even tearful. Some, but by no means all, women return not to the resolution phase but to the plateau stage after orgasm and, with repeated stimulation, are able to orgasm all over again.

Female ejaculation

Research suggests that some women ejaculate fluid when they've had an orgasm through G-spot stimulation. Sexologists who looked into female ejaculation concluded that the fluid was similar to male prostatic fluid and that it comes out of glands near the urethral opening – the female equivalent of the prostate gland. Female ejaculation is still controversial: it's not the same thing as vaginal lubrication and can be confused with urine – sometimes during a strong orgasm, a woman can leak urine because she loses control over her muscles.

Sex on the brain

Before you get physically aroused, you usually perceive something as sexy – the sight of your partner undressing, a horny guy walking by, an explicit film, or the warm breath of another person on your skin. This awakens sexual desire, which in turn triggers the changes in your body that occur when you're aroused.

It all takes place in an area of the brain called the limbic system: this is where we process sensual and emotional information – so touch and taste are dealt with here, alongside thoughts, desires and fantasies. The limbic system converts what's on our minds into physical feelings. In the case of sexual desire, the message being sent out by the brain is to increase blood flow to the genitals, a phenomenon known as psychogenic arousal.

Of course, sexual desire can also be sparked by something purely physical – anything from a long, lingering erotic massage to direct genital stimulation can get our pulses racing and our juices flowing. That's called reflex arousal, and is far simpler but less common than psychogenic arousal.

The most important erogenous zone isn't between your legs, but between your ears.

During real sexual arousal, reflex and psychogenic arousal work together to create the physical symptoms of desire: without them, we'd never get anywhere. Generally, men work more on the reflex arousal: keep stroking his penis in the right way for long enough and he's almost certain to have an orgasm. But for women, you can be doing all the right things physically and she can still get distracted and lose sensitivity if there's no psychological stimulus.

When we experience climax, we release endorphins – the 'happy hormones' that flood through our veins when we're in love or lying in the sun. They're a bit like opiates and latch onto these things we've got called opiate receptors; this is what gives us that rush of pleasure when we have an orgasm.

dirty flirting

Flirting – the art of enticing a potential lover into finding us attractive – is one of the most enjoyable parts of the dating game, and can put the spark back into long-term relationships, too. We're all fluent in body language, even if we're not aware of it on a conscious level. If we manipulate our gestures, our facial expressions and our postures, we can send out messages that say 'I'm interested in you.' These subtle techniques will do the groundwork for you before you even think about using a chat-up line.

Flirt with your...mouth

The mouth is a real hotspot because you're going to use it a) to chat each other up and b) to kiss each other. The lips become redder and larger when we're sexually aroused, which explains the popularity of red lipstick! Licking or wetting your lips or planting them in a pre-kiss position can be sexy, but make sure you don't overdo it.

Flirt with your...bum

When you pass someone you fancy at a party or a nightclub, lightly brush past his or her bottom – it's a highly sexual gesture but, so long as the touch is brief, a non-invasive one. This works best in informal, relaxed situations. Definitely not one for the office unless you want a sexual harassment lawsuit slapped on your desk!

Flirt with your...torso

The extent to which someone mirrors you is a good measure of the rapport you have. So, face the person you're dating with your upper body. If his or her chest position, posture and movements mirror yours, you're onto a winner.

Flirt with your...legs

Women and men tend to point with their feet to the person they're looking at. Try discreetly stroking your thigh, as this subtly invites your partner to do the same. If you're a woman, dangling one high-heeled shoe seductively over the edge of your foot will have him as transfixed as by a hypnotist's watch.

Flirt with your...eyes

It can be tempting to stare at the object of your affection, but that's not sexy. Hold a gaze for 3 seconds or so, break away, look up, and see if you are still being watched. But don't linger – leave him or her still wanting more. Move your eyes slowly down and appreciate, without focusing on one body part – women hate it when men speak to their breasts and men feel intimidated when women stare at their crotch. The key is to create an air of mystery and allure. When we're aroused, our pupils naturally expand, or dilate. This also happens when we're in dim light (the pupils swell to let more light in). Another excuse to let your partner only see you in candlelight!

Flirt with your...shoulders

There's a theory that shoulders remind men of breasts, because they're round and smooth. A top that slides away to reveal your bare shoulders will leave him wanting more. Women consistently say broad shoulders are attractive in men, so for optimum sex appeal men should try sitting with their shoulders back and their arms apart, which also signifies openness and approachability.

Flirt with your...arms

Arms reflect the difference between the male and female body in an easily visible and not massively sexual way. In a woman they reveal softness and femininity. In a man, a strongly veined forearm can be incredibly arousing. To draw attention to your arms, accessorise with an eye-catching bracelet or – if you're a man – a chunky diver's watch. Showing the insides of your wrists signifies approachability and vulnerability. Conversely, folding your arms or pinning them to your sides sends out 'don't approach me' signals.

Flirt with your...hair

When people play with their hair, they subconsciously mimic how they like to be handled by others – so, someone who strokes out his or her long hair is hoping for the same kind of gentle, indulgent attention in bed. You can hide behind long hair and use it as a curtain for coquettish glances. Guys with short hair can draw attention to their hair and eyeline by massaging their hair at the temples.

Kissing with Confidence

The lips have the thinnest and most sensitive skin on the human body, and stimulating them is a shortcut to a state of intense arousal. Kissing is among the most enjoyable and effective methods of foreplay. There's even an ancient Indian theory that the upper lip is connected to the clitoris.

We're all guilty, however, of neglecting kissing once we're in long-term relationships. Perhaps we only kiss deeply and passionately when we want intercourse to follow, or we don't bother at all. That's a shame – think back to the thrill of your early sexual experiences when you'd spend hours necking.

That excitement is easy to recapture. Make a pact with each other to kiss passionately for five minutes every day, regardless of whether or not you intend to follow your kissing session with intercourse. Do it in places other than bed – while you're waiting for the bus on the way to work in the morning, on the way home from the chip shop, in the kitchen while you're doing the washing up. Kissing is safe sex, and you can do it in public, so rediscover the pleasure it can bring with these creative kissing techniques.

● Don't just kiss with your lips: with your finger, lightly trace the outline of your partner's lips from top to bottom. Gently hold his or her lower lip

between your finger and thumb, and then take it into your own mouth and suck it – men in particular love this kiss because their skin here is a bit thicker and can take rougher treatment than female skin. It's also hugely sexy to find a woman sexually confident enough to pull a man towards her in such a gesture of raw desire.

● Put your fingers in your partner's mouth and let him suck on them. It's not surprising how sexy this can feel considering that it mimics the movements of sex itself – a hard part of the body being snugly enclosed in a warm, wet, loving space.

● Don't be scared to breathe each other's breath. Make an airtight seal with your own and your lover's lips, then inhale deeply.

● Kiss each other's ears: some people don't find the tongue/ear interface erotic, but the ones that do are wild for this wet, noisy, sexy kiss! Start with the ear lobe first – cover your teeth with your lips and gently pull it. If you get a positive reaction, swirl your tongue all over your lover's ear, inside and out. If not, do a vampire kiss, working your way down the neck with a series of sexy little nips and sucking lightly on your lover's skin.

● Just grazing each other's lips is very intimate and teasing. Simply tilt your heads from side to side and let your breath mingle. Lick your partner's lips slowly, with the very tip of your tongue, then blow on them, creating a different sensation between warm and cool; this makes already sensitive lips the most tingly zone in the body. Sigh while you're there, showing you're aroused, but don't really let any word out. Because this kiss is only a taste of what's to come, it'll make you both hungry for more.

Sometimes the lightest kiss is the sexiest.

● The endorphins that you release when you're aroused actually block pain receptors, so be bold – bite and snap at each other when you're kissing during foreplay. Men especially say they prefer a slightly aggressive touch when they're kissing as a prelude to sex.

● You can kiss with body parts other than your lips. Take a tip from the Eskimos and nuzzle each other's noses. Rub from side to side, up and down and use the tip of your nose to caress your lover all over his or her scalp, face and neck. Inhale deeply as you kiss, showing your partner you're so aroused that you just want to breathe in every inch of his or her skin.

● Eyelash kisses are soft, subtle and intimate – just flutter your eyelashes against your lover's skin. This is a lovely way to wake your partner up for an early morning lovemaking session!

● Treat the areas your partner likes you to stroke and caress to a long, lingering kiss. If your dry hands can give pleasure, think what your lips and tongue will be able to achieve.

● Take your partner's upper lip between yours while he or she does the same to you with your lower lip, making a kind of lip layered sandwich. Alternate soft nuzzling with tender sucking. This draws more blood to the lips making them extra sensitive.

● Have a cup of tea or hot fruit infusion and alternate with an ice cube for an interesting twist. Avoid coffee, which can be quite an overpowering smell (unless you're both drinking it).

● Kiss each other all over, not just on your lips. One of the best ways to discover new erogenous zones on each other is to kiss every inch of your lover's body – you never quite know what effect you might have!

● Wet your lips with a spirit or liqueur like whisky or sambuca, and challenge your partner to guess what it is.

● Try butterfly kisses – lots of little, dry kisses all over the face and any other part of the body you can access.

● Lead with your tongue, placing it on your partner's lower lip and drawing the rest of the mouth in towards you. Waggle your tongue quickly in each other's mouths and have little sword fights when you're in there. This kiss can be quite aggressively sexy.

● Tickle the roof of your partner's mouth with your tongue. Taste all of your partner's mouth – this is a very erotic, intimate kiss that says 'I want every inch of you.'

● Use each other's mouths to recreate the motions of sex, with lots of thrusting – it can be especially stimulating if the woman's the one doing the thrusting as this reverses the roles of intercourse. She slips her tongue between his loosely closed lips and slides it in and out. To enjoy this technique to the best effect, try it when you're actually in the thrusting part of making love in the missionary position.

● If you do moan while you're snogging, your voice creates a vibration that will be felt all over your partner's body like an electric current. It's subtle so it'll probably be a subconscious feeling, which is great.

● Finally, brush and floss your teeth every day: you'll kiss with much more confidence if you don't have worries about bad breath preying on your mind. It's worth going to a dental hygienist once every six months or so to troubleshoot problems before they start.

2

please Yourself

techniques for Women

Masturbation is not only a fabulous (and free) way to pass a few spare minutes, it's also the best way of getting to know your own body and sexual preferences – and there's no better starting point for sensational sex than that.

It used to be thought that it was possible to get addicted to a little bit of self-love, that nice girls didn't do it, and even that it made you go blind. Thankfully, it's now acknowledged that nice girls *do* masturbate and that a girl needs to know what turns her on before she can enjoy sex with a man. Let's face it – once you can do it yourself, you can train him to do it.

For first-timers

If you've never masturbated before, or you've never had an orgasm, set aside an evening when you won't be disturbed to make it happen. Slowly undress yourself, or slip into a negligée or lingerie that makes you feel sexy. Light your room with candles and, if it helps you relax, have half a glass of wine. Think about what turns you on and read a sexy book or watch a movie you find

Learning the secrets of solo sex could be one of the most valuable things you ever do for yourself.

arousing as your fingers do the walking. Above all, remember that tonight is about exploring your body and there's no pressure for anything to happen. If you don't reach a climax tonight, what's the hurry? You've got the rest of your life to try again until you do.

Indulge yourself

As with intercourse, you could use a little foreplay. It's totally normal to fantasise during masturbation – most of us need something extra to get us there. You can enhance your fantasies during masturbation

– for example, if you're using thoughts of sex with your partner to get you off, wrap a scarf covered in his aftershave around your neck, or wear nothing but one of his shirts. Play music that you listen to when you're making love to him or watch a film that you enjoyed together before – or during – the last time you made out. Make your foreplay-for-one physical as well as psychological. Trace your fingers all over your body before you touch yourself intimately. Pinch your nipples, let your hair trail over your shoulder, bite your lips. Trace a silk scarf or feather over your body, waking up every nerve ending on your skin. The more sensually alive you feel, the more orgasmic you're likely to be when you eventually start stimulating your genitals.

Your clitoris is so sensitive that it can become numb and unresponsive if it isn't well lubricated. There's a slight design fault in the human female: your own natural juices come from your vagina, so if you're lying on your back, it's hard to transfer this moisture to your clitoris without losing some of it along the way. As your body learns to respond to your touch, you'll produce more natural lubrication, but there's no harm in helping things along with a little water-based sex lubricant. Apply generously – it's better to overdo it than underdo it. You'll know if you've used too much because you'll feel less, not more, sensation; some degree of friction is needed to reach orgasm.

Get comfortable

There are innumerable ways of getting yourself off, but if you are new to the pleasures of solo sex, try some of the following, easy-to-master techniques...

Sitting or lying back The most popular way for women to masturbate is to sit or lie back on a bed or chair, legs spread or crossed. This is the position for you if you like to watch a dirty movie or read erotica while you masturbate.

Pressing the soles of your feet together will increase tension in your crotch area. Start by stroking yourself through your knickers – if you're very sensitive that might even be enough. Use the middle and index finger of whichever hand you write with. Pull your labia apart at the top to increase exposure of the nerve endings that surround the clitoris. Try stroking it up and down, circling it or lightly flicking it repeatedly. To begin with, it's a good idea to stick to a steady rhythm, but when you're more familiar with the way your clitoris responds, you can tease yourself by stopping and starting the stimulation, staving off orgasm until you just can't take any more. Some people increase stimulation as they approach orgasm – you'll instinctively know what's right for you.

Arse upwards Another popular way for women to masturbate is to lie face down on the bed and rub against something: a pillow, a hairbrush, a vibrator, your hand or anything that tickles your fancy. You also get to 'hump' as you would during intercourse, which can be a psychological as well as a physical incentive to reach orgasm, especially if you're fantasising about making love to someone while you masturbate. What's more, there's the benefit of having your whole body rub up and down the bed, providing friction for sensitive areas like your nipples, stomach and pubic area – parts of the body that are often treated to skin-on-skin contact during sexual intercourse. If you like this position, try approaching yourself from behind and see how different that feels.

Knowing that it's your own hand giving you all this pleasure can be liberating and exhilarating. But if you find, conversely, that it takes the edge off your pleasure, you may find it much more of a turn-on to sit on your hands until they go numb, thus creating the illusion that it's someone else's hand doing the work...

Hydrotherapy Many women's first experience of orgasm happens in the shower – held against the clitoris for a minute or two, a soft jet of water can produce results so pleasurable you'll be clawing at the shower curtain. As long as the water isn't too hot and you don't have the shower turned up full blast, this is a perfectly safe way to masturbate. A lot of women enjoy spa baths for the same reason, but be warned: the water here can be a little too powerful, and you run the risk of desensitising yourself so your clitoris can only respond to rapidly whooshing jets of water – and the chances of your partner being able to recreate that particular sensation with his hands is slim to say the least. It's not a good idea to direct a jet of water directly up your vagina; powerful blasts can tear the delicate skin in there, and also carry a risk of upsetting your personal pH balance,

Never underestimate the effects of a gentle jet of warm water.

which could cause a nasty infection. A much more gentle variation on this theme is to trickle water over the clitoris – the slow drip-drip-drip movement can be a sedate build-up to an amazing climax!

With a dildo or vibrator If you normally concentrate on your clitoris when you masturbate, and you only use your hands, try masturbating with a dildo inside you. Because the muscles of your vaginal wall contract furiously during orgasm, it's a completely different sensation when there's something inside you.

If, after repeated attempts, you can't bring yourself to orgasm with your hands or a dildo, experiment with a vibrator. It couldn't be simpler – all you need to do is to part your legs, apply the vibrator to your clitoris and wait for the fireworks. A good vibrator will deliver the goods in a matter of minutes, so if you're busy busy busy then this is the method for you! Another excellent position is to kneel with the vibrator clamped between your legs – when climax comes, you'll literally go weak at the knees. Set it on a low speed to begin with, as over-enthusiastic first-timers don't realise just how fast and powerful modern sex toys are, and can end up doing themselves more harm than good, bruising the very parts they're trying to stimulate.

Once you've experienced an orgasm, you're much more likely to do so again. Your body now knows exactly what it's capable of and wants to get there again! So next time you masturbate, try using your hands, or stroking your clitoris with the vibrator while it's switched off, training your body to respond to all types of touch. If you become dependent on sex toys to reach orgasm, you won't be able to fully enjoy your own or your partner's touch during foreplay and intercourse.

techniques for men

Ensure you have total privacy and no distractions – you'll need at least half an hour for the advanced techniques in this section. Relax and clear your mind of worries about work, your relationship, the football score – concentrate on your body and what it's capable of. Stretch every muscle in your body, paying particular attention to your back and pelvis; circle your pelvis and arch your back so that all your tensions and stresses are released. Sexual energy can't flow properly through a tense body.

Have a bath or shower, shave and apply aftershave – prepare your body as though you were going on a first date. You deserve it. Undress completely and lie back on your bed. Treat yourself to a little foreplay – stroke, press and tickle all the erogenous zones you can reach. Use massage oil on your chest if it turns you on.

You're probably used to using any lubricant that comes to hand – whether that's baby lotion, shower gel or even cooking oil. There's no question that masturbation is a smoother, more pleasant experience when there's less friction between the palm of your hand and your penis. If you've never tried a commercial lubricant, you'll be amazed at the difference. Water-based products are long-lasting and will come nearer to mimicking the natural moisture of the inside of a vagina than anything else.

Keep your hand in

Most men masturbate either sitting or lying down – if that's your preferred position, try this new technique. Begin with one hand over the head of your erection and pull the skin down towards the base, so it's totally taut and every vein and nerve ending is exposed and vulnerable to your touch. Now use your other hand to trace along those veins and to stroke that skin. For a variation on this theme, twist the skin at the base of the penis – your cries of ecstasy should give new meaning to the phrase 'twist and shout'!

● You can also rhythmically thrust your penis against the bed, plunging it into a pillow or into a snug fold in the bedsheets. If you're lying face down, prop your face and chest up on some pillows so that you can breathe properly. For extra sensation, hold your penis lightly as you thrust, and squeeze your legs together to enhance the experience.

● Make believe it's someone else's hand giving you pleasure – invest in a pair of gloves. Leather gloves will feel luxuriously warm and soft, while rubber surgical or hairdresser's ones will feel wonderfully kinky; but don't even think about using gloves without a generous amount of lubricant... This is one place you really don't want a friction burn.

● Condoms aren't just for contraception. Ribbed varieties have the 'grooves' on the outside for the woman's pleasure, but you can also turn them inside out and slip them on before masturbating for a completely new sensation. To make the condom feel even more delicious, fill it with a thick, water-based lubricant at the tip before you start. The jelly will liquefy as it warms up with the heat from your hand and the friction you're causing and melt gradually along the shaft of your penis.

● The bath or shower is second only to the bed and sofa as a popular place to masturbate. Hair conditioner makes an excellent lubricant (and will leave your pubic hair silky soft as an added bonus!). Try directing the shower jet on your perineum to stimulate your prostate gland.

● Many men fantasise about masturbating in public but this is one fantasy that really shouldn't be enacted on the beach or in the park. You don't want to get prosecuted for indecent exposure! A much safer way to indulge 'public' fantasies at home is to masturbate just out of sight, with the window open.

● Try not to get into a rut: if you always use pornography when you masturbate, see if you can climax without it, on fantasy alone. If you tend not to use pornography, try it – it could tap into sexual desires and fantasies you never knew you had. If you usually remain silent during sex, talk to yourself as you get yourself off. Tell yourself how good you feel. Let your body take over and say whatever comes into your head. Don't feel self-conscious about the words that come out of your mouth – who's going to tell? Shouting loudly as you're about to orgasm feels empowering and the strain on your voice can enhance the physical pleasure. As you get near, behave as your body wants you to: jerk about and thrust your pelvis.

● Don't be in a hurry to clean yourself up. Have tissues or a towel to hand so you can lie there for as long as you like, thinking about the experience you've just had. Notice how long it takes for your breathing and pulse rate to calm down. How long is it before the sensitive head of your penis feels OK to touch again? Do you feel happy, tired, relaxed?

On and on: how masturbation can make a longer-lasting lover

Because men typically learn to masturbate while they're still living at home with their parents, they tend to do it as quickly as they possibly can – the fear of being discovered means men are conditioned to get it over with before someone walks in and catches them at it. While the ability to reach orgasm in under a minute is useful when you can hear footsteps on the stairs and a key in the front door, it isn't going to endear you to future sexual partners. It is possible, however, to learn how to delay ejaculation.

Typically, your breathing becomes faster and shallower the nearer you are to climaxing. Because this is a natural reflex, you probably don't think to challenge it. But by controlling something as simple as your breathing patterns you can learn to control, delay or even avoid ejaculation and orgasm. As you feel yourself approaching climax – but well before you've reached your own 'point of no return' – stop touching yourself for a moment or two. The second you feel your erection begin to subside, resume

Through masturbation, you can teach yourself to delay orgasm by minutes, even hours.

stimulation. Keep this up for as long as you can bear to, and with practice you should be able to hold off orgasm for three or four times longer than normal. This trick can be incorporated into intercourse by withdrawing from your partner and concentrating on her pleasure for a few moments until you feel safe to resume penetration.

After you've mastered this technique, you're ready for an ancient Taoist take on masturbation that promises an orgasm like you've never known it before. After masturbating for several minutes, just before you're about to come, breathe in deeply, squeeze your PC muscles (the ones you use to stop and start the flow when you're urinating, see page 15) and instead of thinking about your semen spurting out of your body, visualise it turning back in on itself, travelling down the penis, up the spine and dispersing through your body. Men who successfully complete this exercise report full-body orgasms, the after-effects of which can still be felt hours later. For further climax-delaying techniques, turn to pages 121–22.

Watching each Other

Now you both know how to get the most out of solo sex, isn't it time you showed off your new skills to an appreciative audience? Watching each other masturbate is a nerve-racking but educational, intimate and erotic experience.

There's a certain performance aspect to this that can be daunting – especially if masturbation is how you normally reach orgasm and you're not coming through intercourse. If you're nervous, enjoy a glass of wine together first, or just lie holding and touching each other for a while.

The easiest way to 'perform' for each other is to sit opposite your lover with your legs spread. This not only affords you a great view of your partner's genitalia and what they're doing to it, but also lets you look into their eyes so that even though you're not actually having intercourse, you can share each other's orgasms by maintaining eye contact as you touch yourselves. The sight of each other will also turn you both on – you're more likely to reach orgasm if you have a great view of their naked body and face as they journey towards climax. It's also fun to turn each other on by drawing attention to your sexiest body parts. For example, you could lightly pinch your nipples to make them erect and darker if you know that excites him, or – guys – you can flex your arms if you know that's what she likes about your body.

Actions speak louder than words, and watching your lover masturbate will show you exactly what it takes to get him or her off. Notice the speed they move at; whether they stop and start or use one continuous movement; how long it takes them; and if there are any parts they touch that you haven't thought of. For example, perhaps your boyfriend cups his balls with one hand while stroking the shaft of his penis with the other, or maybe your girlfriend spends ages stroking her labia before she progresses to her clitoris. You can use these tips in mutual masturbation, foreplay and intercourse.

For a real turn-on, masturbate side by side in front of a mirror.

You can reach out and caress each other if you like, but you must stay away from each other's genitals, otherwise you will defeat the object of this exercise. Try sucking each other's fingers or reaching over to kiss each other. Don't be afraid to ask questions: 'Why does that feel good?' 'Are you close to coming?' 'Is looking at me turning you on?' Or tell each other that it's making you horny – say things like: 'Your face looks beautiful when you're about to come,' or 'Your cock looks really sexy.'

If you're really shy, you could even sit back to back to begin with until you get used to the idea of sharing this private experience. Or perhaps, if you're used to masturbating on your back with your legs apart, you could lay in your partner's lap while he or she watches.

3

Just for Starters

Sexy Stripping

There are times when you're so hot for each other you've ripped all your clothes off before you've even closed the front door. While it's true that tearing off tights with your teeth signifies passion, the fine art of sexy stripping is one worth learning – for both of you.

But before you settle in for a striptease, try to create as sexy an environment as possible. If possible, save the bedroom for sleeping and making love – if you spend hours there every day doing mundane things like ironing or watching television, you'll find it hard to turn your mind to more erotic pastimes. It's important that you both find your lovemaking space peaceful and sexy.

Setting the scene

The easiest ways to create the boudoir you want are through colour and light. The best colour for a bedroom is red – recent research found that rich, orangey reds raise testosterone levels. Make sure you're comfortable with the lighting level. Women often say they're happier with the lights out, but many men – who rely largely on images for arousal – will think a lot more of a girl who's confident enough to enjoy sex with the lights on. Compromise with low-level lighting. Candles are the most conducive. A couple of really large candles will create a soft glow over the

Your bedroom should be a retreat – a special, intimate place for both of you.

whole room while lots of tiny tealights will cast a flattering light on your skin. Or why not tie a string of fairylights to your bedposts?

It's key to tread the fine line between having things around you that turn you on and surrounding yourself with distractions. So make sure pictures are arty and subtle, and save family photographs for the mantelpiece in the living room – do you really want to have sex underneath a portrait of granny and grandpa at their golden wedding celebrations? If you like to make love to music, make sure it's something you both agree on – have a stack of favourite CDs by the bed. Set up the stereo so that you each have a speaker on your side of the bed, or put the speakers at a low level so you can feel the vibrations when you turn the music up loud!

Now you're ready to get naked! Put on some music that makes you feel sexy, something with a slow beat and maybe some steamy lyrics. If you're feeling a bit cheeky, slow big band-style numbers such as 'The Stripper' are excellent scene-setters. Songs played in strip clubs tend to be slowly syncopated dance anthems or rocky eighties-style ballads.

Strip tips for her

Putting on a striptease is largely about catering to your partner's fantasies, but you've got to be comfortable with what you're doing, too. Boost your confidence

Nothing arouses a man like seeing the woman he loves peel off layer after layer of clothing in a show just for him.

by rehearsing a few times, and do whatever it takes to make you feel good about your body, whether that's using fake tan, body oil or shimmering make-up to look and feel your best. Each tip in this step-by-step guide to the perfect striptease comes from professional strippers, lap dancers or blue movie actresses. Follow these rules and you can't go wrong. This is a visual feast, so add to the excitement by insisting on a 'no touching' rule, which a lot of actual strip clubs do enforce (although there's no rule to say he can't touch *himself* if he's getting horny just watching…).

● A good striptease requires careful planning. The way you put your clothes on will affect the way you take them off again. Are you hoping to finish your striptease with intercourse, and if so, are you planning to make love partially clothed? If this is the case, you're going to have to slip your panties on over the top of your suspenders.

● Begin by taking your hair down or, if it's short, ruffling it to show you're relaxing and ready for fun. Run your hands over your clothes, showing him how much you enjoy the feel of the different fabrics against your skin.

● Shoes should either be taken off first or left on till last. If you're wearing long boots, slide your hands up and down the leather before unzipping them slowly and seductively. Stilettos should be dangled on the edge of your toe, just out of his reach, before being kicked off out of sight.

● The more buttons, zips and buckles you have to undo to get out of your clothes, the better. You want your striptease to be tantalisingly slow and drawn out. As you undress, watch what you're doing. Smile and look up at your partner to check he's enjoying himself as much as you are.

● Skirts should be slipped off seductively. Slide trousers slowly down and step out of them one leg at a time. Keep turning around as you undress, giving him a great angle of every inch of your body.

● Tights just aren't sexy – it's virtually impossible to wriggle out of a pair of control tights and maintain your allure. So wear hold-ups or, if you don't have the thighs of a young gazelle (which most of us don't!), stockings and suspenders.

● Take off your bra really slowly. Lower the straps from your shoulders one by one. He's waiting for the first glimpse of your nipples, so don't disappoint. If you're wearing a push-up bra, and you don't want the contrast between your pneumatic, pert puppies and your natural, less-than-flawless breasts to alarm him, stretch your arms above your head to make your tits look perkier, or push them together with your arms and bend over to make them look bigger.

● Peel off your panties by hooking your thumbs in the front of the waistband. Then peek down the front, look at him, turn round and let him see your arse as you roll them slowly down and ultimately step out of them leg by leg. If you're feeling really wild, sniff them before waving them under his nose and draping them across his face.

Strip tips for him

Undressing isn't something men traditionally pay much attention to, most preferring to whip off their clothes as soon as possible. But a slow, sexy striptease could be the secret weapon in your seduction routine. These tips, provided by male strippers, will drive her wild without you having to lay a finger on her.

● You may not have a wardrobe of luxurious lingerie at your disposal (then again, you may), but that needn't stop you thinking about what you wear. Socks should be plain and dark, and most women agree that the most fashionable and flattering underpants are cotton boxer-briefs, also in dark plain colours.

● Whatever you do, take off your shoes and socks first. There's nothing more undignified than a man standing there in just his socks. Apart from anything else this shows consideration – you're not just ripping your clothes off ready to jump on her. Sit on the edge of the bed while you take them off.

● Think about what your best features are: if you've got great legs, begin with your trousers. If you're not overconfident about your chest and shoulders, leave your shirt hanging open – the teasing glimpse of your torso will get her excited.

● Cater to her fantasies by dressing up in a uniform – think fireman, policeman or soldier. Cover your body in oil and wear a leather thong to give her an extra thrill. For more tips on dressing up for fantasy fun, turn to pages 128–29.

● The more formal the clothes are, the sexier your striptease will be. Think about it: can you imagine wriggling sexily out of a tracksuit? If you have to take a jumper off, resist the temptation to cross your arms behind your neck and yank it over. Rather, cross your arms in front of your body and slowly peel it off.

● If you've got an erection, take your time to undo your belt buckle, then turn to the side so she can see how excited you are.

● Keep one item of clothing on. If you're wearing a tie, rub it along your shoulders and then let it hang down so that the ends are caressing your nipples.

Undressing each other

● Guys, learn how to unhook a woman's bra – endless fumbling can spoil the mood. If you need to, practise while she's out on one of her bras tied round a chair back.

● Girls, learn how to undo a man's belt with real decisiveness. It's a tiny gesture, but one that shows how keen you are to see what's behind the buckle.

● Unbutton the other person's shirt, slowly. Even taking off a coat can be really intimate.

● Using your teeth to tear off your lover's clothing is incredibly passionate – and remember, shirt buttons that pop off can be sewn back on again!

turn-ons for him

Men may think they don't want any foreplay, but that's because they've never had their bodies lingered over in the following ways:

● Don't go straight for his genitals. Men who've never had their bodies caressed and cuddled in the run up to the main event don't realise this adds fuel to the fire.

● Drip candle wax all over him – test it on your own skin first so you know what you're doing. The sharp shock of hot wax on his skin will awaken his nerves and make his whole body tingle in anticipation. There's also something incredibly sexy about a woman who is, quite literally, playing with fire.

● Bite him. Men like being bitten during foreplay because it displays aggressive sexuality on the part of the woman.

● Leave a Polaroid camera in surprise locations – under his pillow, tucked into his briefcase – to let him know you're in the mood to play. Men are more dependent on visual stimuli than women, and he'll love the notion that you're his very own centrefold.

● Feel him up through his pants or trousers. Press his perineum. Some men can be nervous about being stimulated so close to their anus (even though they love the feeling it gives them) so having a layer of fabric between your finger and his skin can feel safer; what's more, this spot is so sensitive that direct, firm stimulation can sometimes be a little too intense for comfort.

● Drive him wild by holding his balls in the palm of your hand and gently rolling them around. Alternate this by playing 'pat-a-cake' with a flaccid penis – he'll be anything but putty in your hands.

● Don't be afraid to be heavy handed. Men have thicker skin than women and require a firmer touch to become aroused. Ask him if he wants you to go harder or softer as you caress him.

● Rouse him (and arouse him) by taking his morning glory erection in your mouth. He won't know if he's awake or dreaming…

● Trail your breasts all over his body – use your nipples to make swirling patterns on his skin. Or take him in your arms when you're topless and use your hands to massage his head while it nestles in your chest. He won't be able to resist nuzzling your breasts.

● Hold his penis still in your hand while you stroke him everywhere else. This will desensitise him and make him go on for longer. The longer you delay penetrative sex, the more explosive it'll be.

● Break up the routine. Go down on him before you've done the usual touchy feely preamble, and only after he's hard move on to the usual foreplay.

● Have to hand a radiator-warmed towel and an ice cube. Place each on his chest in turn, holding them there until he can't take any more. Ten seconds should have him squirming with anticipation. Repeat this process, working your way down his body until you reach his penis.

● Tighten your thumb and forefinger around the base of his penis, pressing down on his balls. This will limit the blood supply and help you steady his shaft so you can masturbate him more vigorously and longer than before.

● There's a small tube that runs just under the skin, halfway up the scrotum to the base of his penis. Running your fingers lightly along this line indirectly massages the urethra – a super-sensitive spot that can register intense pleasure.

Making safe sex sexy

Until you've both been given a clean bill of sexual health, there's no excuse not to use a condom. One of the reasons we don't always practise safe sex is the dreaded 'condom moment' between foreplay and intercourse where the action has to stop while we struggle with the condom wrapper. But, with a little know-how and a lot of style, it's easy to make putting on a condom an erotic experience.

Start with a brief genital massage to get him in the mood (see pages 108–9) and make him feel like the experience is a treat, not a chore. Resist the temptation to rip the condom out of its wrapper with your mouth as your teeth could tear the rubber. Squeeze the air out of the 'teat' at the tip of the condom between your thumb and forefinger. Put it on the top of his penis with one hand and roll it down to the base with the other. Don't skip straight to intercourse – give him time to get used to the feel of the condom. Use the same slow, sensuous movements that you did during the genital massage just now, to make the experience as sexy as possible.

Condoms are not only protective but help men to delay climax for longer – good news all round.

Lip service: putting on a condom with your mouth

Use a flavoured one – not only will it make the experience more enjoyable for you, but you can bet he doesn't want to kiss a woman whose mouth tastes of latex. Before you start, take off your lipstick, balm or gloss as it may contain oil, which will break down the latex.

Use your mouth on his penis to make him erect. For a blow-by-blow account of how to do this, see pages 58–60. It's important that your lips are covered by your teeth at all times here – your lips alone won't be strong enough to do the job, and your teeth alone will a) hurt him, and b) damage the condom. Place the teat of the condom between your lips, holding it in place with very light suction. Hold the shaft of his penis in one hand and use your lips to place the condom on the tip of his penis. You might need to use your spare hand to help roll it down for the first centimetre or so, but thereafter use your tongue and lips to push it all the way down. When you get so far you can't accommodate any more of his penis in the back of your throat, take over with your hands.

If you're relying on condoms to protect you from pregnancy and infection, always use one with a Kite mark and an expiry date on the packet. Beware of novelty condoms, which are not designed for contraceptive purposes. If you're practising anal sex, which can be rougher than vaginal sex, use the extra-strong condoms specially manufactured for this purpose.

turn-ons for her

This is the get-her-going guide every man should have. Don't go to bed without it! The first thing you should know is that it takes women, on average, 20 minutes to journey from arousal to orgasm. Men, on the other hand, can come in three minutes flat. It doesn't take a mathematical genius to work out that men need to spend those spare 17 minutes making sure their lover is aroused enough to enjoy intercourse. That pre-sex ritual of stroking, kissing and caressing is known as foreplay – and women can't get enough of it.

Most women want more foreplay, not only because it's an exquisite pastime in its own right, but because it's a physical necessity for good sex. She needs foreplay if she's going to become aroused: without it she won't lubricate sufficiently and she won't be able to accommodate your penis, which is uncomfortable for both of you. It's also a fact that if she's not ready for penetration you can make tiny tears in her vagina, leaving her – and therefore you, as her sexual partner – vulnerable to infection.

The foreplay rules

These are the only tips you'll ever need – follow these guidelines and have her begging for more. There's a whole lifetime of foreplay ideas in the next few pages, but don't make the mistake of trying all of them out in one evening! One variation on the theme per sexual encounter please!

Constant caresses

Touch her even when you don't want sex. That's the best way to make sure her body is constantly primed. Some women come to resent kisses and caresses that only materialise before foreplay. Kiss and touch her in public. This says you're proud to be near her, proud to be with her and you can't take your hands off her, even though you're not about to have sex. Kiss her hand and stroke her hair when you walk past her.

Stealth seduction

The further away from the genitals you begin to touch her, the more surprised and delighted she'll be. Roll her onto her front and trail a scarf over her back. Ironically, you'll find that neglecting obvious erogenous zones like the breasts and clitoris can increase her arousal and sensitivity in those exact areas, as blood flows to the sex organs no matter how she becomes aroused. Surprise her by starting at the feet – suck her toes one by one. Flex your tongue, making it into a little point that darts in between every toe; these tiny spaces are packed with nerve endings and are barely ever touched, making them extra-sensitive. Lick her all over: show her you want all of her, that there's nowhere you're afraid to put your tongue. The small dent in between the top of her buttocks will be particularly responsive to a surprise kiss or lick, and, if you're willing to boldly go, some women love the feel of a tongue on and around the thin, sensitive skin of the anus.

Blow her away

Touch her in ways she's never been touched before, but instead of caressing her with your hands, use your breath. This is the ultimate technique from the 'less is more' school of foreplay. Your hot breath on her inner thighs, neck and stomach, or even gently blowing on her clitoris, can arouse her more than the touch of your hands – the warmth and intimacy of it will melt her.

If you're really in the mood to show off, use your erect penis to tease, tickle and massage her. Ask her to spread her legs, as though you were going to penetrate her, but instead of entering her vagina, use the tip of your penis to trace the outline of her vulva, and lightly to tickle the clitoris. Keep this up for a minute or two and she'll be begging to have you inside her.

Breast intentions

Breasts are highly erogenous zones, but don't approach them first: many women complain that men tend to pay attention to the breasts and genitals at the expense of the rest of their bodies. Tease her by touching the skin around her breasts – on her sides, collarbone and underarms – first. When you do brush against her breasts, do it so lightly it could almost be an accident. Start from the underside of her breast, an area that is often overlooked, and just let her relax into the sensation for a few minutes. And most importantly, leave the nipple till last. She'll be so delighted that she's found a man who doesn't twiddle her nipples as though he were adjusting a radio set, that she'll be desperate for you to caress this sensitive area. If you bite her nipples, do it with your lips covering your teeth. A law of symmetry applies to the female body – repeat every touch on each breast for best results. Rub ice cubes on her nipples to make them stand up and become more sensitive. This will also enhance your viewing pleasure because her breasts will swell slightly, making them fuller and more pert.

Nuzzles and nips

Bite at her ear lobes rather than plunging your tongue into her inner ear. As a rule, women are less likely than men to enjoy aural stimulation because in men, the ears are a site of testosterone (that's why men get hairy ears and women don't). Her skin is thinner and more sensitive than yours. Don't touch her as you want to be touched – if you think you're not being firm enough and that no-one could possibly enjoy such featherlight caresses, she's probably in heaven.

Variety is the spice...

Don't use the same strokes every time – the nerve endings in her body will become accustomed to your touch and she'll lose that highly arousing sensation of never quite knowing where the next touch is coming from. Cover her body in wavy, ever-changing strokes – save steady rhythms for intimate massage (see page 109).

Cleanliness is next to sexiness

Women often say that the most important physical attribute in a man is that he's clean. Poor hygiene, especially in the genital area and the mouth, consistently ranks high in the list of turn-offs. Turning up to bed with unwashed armpits or unbrushed teeth shows her you don't care enough about her – or yourself – to wash! Make a bath or shower into fore-play: not only can bathtime be great fun, but soaping and lathering each other's skin is an easy and informal erotic massage. And it goes without saying that the cleaner you both are, the more confident you'll be to explore every inch of each other's bodies. Cleanliness is an absolute must if you're going to progress to anal play, and very much recommended if oral sex, anal play or toe-sucking is on the menu.

To increase the intimacy, lie together and try to coordinate your breathing.

Join in her grooming routine: if she usually applies body lotion after a bath or shower, offer to rub it into her skin, starting at her feet and working upwards, massaging the lotion into her skin in brisk, firm strokes. Brush her hair, whether she's got a short boyish crop or locks as long as Rapunzel's. Some brushes are designed to massage with bristles that stimulate the scalp: ask your local hairdresser or chemist to recommend one. Give her a facial. Cover every inch of her face with your fingertips. Trace from her eyes, all round her lips, around her jawline and back to her lips, then put your finger in her mouth. Shave her legs, which will turn both of you on.

Abstinence makes the heart grow fonder

If you're getting into too much of a routine, deny yourselves penetrative sex for a week, and instead make a point of spending half an hour a day in bed indulging in the stroking and caressing you'd usually save for foreplay. It is often when you're enjoying the techniques for their own sake, rather than as a prelude to intercourse, that you get really creative and discover new ways to tease and please each other.

Mental foreplay

Prepare the groundwork by putting her mind to thoughts of sex before you even lay a finger on her. Sounds like too much hassle? Look at it this way: the more sexually charged she is by the time she gets home, the deeper into the stages of psychogenic arousal she'll be and the less actual physical foreplay you'll have to do. Now are you convinced?

● Send her a huge bunch of flowers with a sex toy or another treat hidden inside the bouquet.

● Buy her underwear and tell her you want to see her in it – the more luxurious the better.

● Leave a smutty voicemail on her mobile or work phone, letting her know what you want to do when she gets home.

● Slip a dirty book into her handbag and bookmark a particularly explicit page – attach a post-it note asking her to help you make your fantasy come true.

Afterplay

Modern man has mainly been educated about foreplay, but what about afterplay? In general, immediately after sex, men tend to feel such a release of tension that all their sexual and emotional cravings are satisfied through their orgasm. Women, who don't always come through penetrative sex alone, are programmed differently. Sometimes women find that they need more, not less, attention after sex, and because they're emotionally charged, with high levels of oestrogen in their bodies, they can feel needy and vulnerable. Insensitive post-sex behaviour on his part can alter her whole perception of the sexual experience. Follow this advice and make sure the cool-down is as much fun as the warm-up...

● Afterplay is especially important following 'quickie' sex where you've both been too sexually charged to linger over foreplay. Even if the sex is over in less than five minutes, there's no rules to say you can't have some pillow talk and tender stroking as you 'come down' from the high of your orgasms.

● Make sure you have tissues and a waste bin to hand. When a man withdraws from a woman and rushes off to the bathroom to dispose of the condom or clean himself up after sex it can feel like a rejection. Offer to gently wipe her clean too.

● If you know you feel grouchy immediately after sex, finish off in a man-on-top position and just lie there inside her for a while, holding her, not saying anything, while your erection subsides.

● Last, but by no means least, kiss her, hold her and tell her how much you enjoyed making love – this is the only unbreakable rule!

Mutual Masturbation

Learning how to pleasure your partner with your hands is easier than you think – it's a vital part of foreplay and a must-have skill for men and women who can't always achieve orgasm through penetrative sex (or who want to add variety to their climaxes).

How to masturbate a woman

This is often the most important part of your foreplay routine. You can use these techniques to prepare a woman for intercourse or as a treat in its own right.

Women have varying tastes: some like you to touch them all over before you go for the genitals, others prefer you to start there so they're wet before the rest of foreplay. Some get the most pleasure when you begin with the very lightest of stroking movements, others would rather that you dive right in with fast, firm stimulation. If you don't know what her preferences are, ask her, or suggest she uses her hand to guide you. Watching her masturbate will also give you a good idea of the kind of speed and pressure she likes.

Just as you wouldn't kiss a girl if you hadn't given your teeth a good brush, be sure to wash your hands and check your nails and fingers for snags and calluses. Ladies are more sensitive to touch than men, and nowhere more so than the genitals. If your hands are rough or callused, borrow some of her hand lotion – she'll thank you for it.

The hands-on experience will be much smoother and sexier for both of you if you use a lubricant. Don't take it personally if she doesn't get wet – all sorts of factors, such as where she is in her cycle, whether she's had a drink, and how stressed or nervous she is, can affect a woman's natural lubrication. Use a water-based product rather than silicone or oil-based lotions, which can upset the delicate pH balance of the

Learning how to touch a woman in all the right places is a skill no man should be without.

vagina. You can also use your own saliva to keep things running smoothly if you don't have any lube to hand. Apply the lubricant to your fingertips and warm it by rubbing them together before you touch her. If you drip the lubricant directly onto her clitoris, she'll squeal from shock as well as delight!

Different positions for masturbating a woman

● Lie down behind her, so you can kiss her neck and play with her breasts at the same time. This can feel very nurturing and intimate, but you may need to use one of your hands to balance.

● Lie on top of her, much as you would for the missionary position – again, you'll need at least one hand to lean on. However, you can kiss and talk to her throughout and all she has to do is lie back and enjoy the experience.

● Sit her down on the edge of the bed or a chair and kneel between her legs. This is a great position because you can use both hands and progress to oral, too. She might feel vulnerable because you can see all of her body – but you can tell her how sexy she really looks.

● From the back – she leans over as she would for doggy-style sex. This is perfect for quickie fingering sessions in unusual locations (like the worktop or over a balcony on holiday), and gives you easy access to her anus and perineum if that's what she likes.

How to do it

Your wrist will get tired, so rest it on her pubic bone (the fleshy triangle covered by her pubic hair) or thigh, depending on the direction from which you're approaching her. This way, you won't have the whole weight of your arm bearing down and will be better equipped to deliver the lighter strokes that women prefer. The golden rule here is definitely that less is more. Use your front two fingers to slide down along the inner lips on either side of the clitoral bud. You can't actually pick it up and squeeze it, but you can bring your fingers oh-so-slightly closer together as they slide over it.

Start with an almost non-existent stroke; if she wants more, she can ask for it.

Some women like you gradually to build up sensation around the clitoris rather than going straight for it. Lightly trace your finger in little circles all round the clit until she's begging for you to touch it. Or start by trailing your forefinger, middle finger and ring finger up along the bottom of the labia – this is a very gentle yet effective way to stimulate all over her genitals at once.

If you've got both hands free, slide a couple of fingers inside her as she's about to come – it feels much nicer for her to have something inside her as she orgasms. Your four fingers should be resting flat over her pubic bone, lightly pressuring and stroking this area, while your thumb caresses her clitoris. Thumbs are larger and fleshier than fingers, which is nice for her if her clitoris is especially sensitive.

To stimulate her G-spot, slide a well-lubed finger up her vagina and beckon towards the front (this works best if you're behind her). Can you feel a little pea-sized nodule about halfway up? Bingo.

Getting to grips with your man

A good hand job is worth perfecting because, unlike penetrative or oral sex, you can take it anywhere. Many women are nervous about using their hands to bring their partners to orgasm, for the very valid reason that he's been practising on himself since he was a teenager – how are we ever going to compete or catch up with that? The beauty of the hand job is that it's not instinctive, it's a skill you can learn. Practise the following tips on a lifelike dildo, even a cucumber if you need to, and learn to enjoy it.

Choose your position

The position is key: you'll be approaching his penis from directions he could never manage himself – and believe me, they've all been tried. The number one tried-and-tested position is as follows: he sits or lies on the edge of the bed, propped up by pillows, while you sit or kneel between his legs. You see exactly what you're doing, and you've got good access to his balls. Make eye contact with him and gaze at his erection as though it's the most beautiful thing ever.

All the two-handed techniques described in this chapter are designed to be carried out from this position. But you can vary the theme with different degrees of sitting or lying down, or by changing locations – chairs and stairways being two good ideas.

The alternative is to sit down beside or behind him. This is a great position for when you want to do it quickly. You might not have excellent access to his penis, but if you're in an unusual situation, this alone will be enough of a turn-on for him. You can also hurry things along by talking dirty in his ear or pressing on his perineum.

How to do it

Don't be shy about using lubricant to help things along – men tend to when they masturbate, as a dry hand moving quickly against a dry penis causes the wrong kind of friction. Make a big show of warming the lubricant between your palms, giving him a taste of the hot hand action that's about to come his way. Take his hands in yours and massage the lube into his penis and balls together – not only will this 'include' him in your manual loveplay, but you'll also get an idea of the kind of strokes and rhythm he wants you to use.

A word about your manicure – long talons can be a real turn-on for a lot of men.

Massage a little lube into your breasts to get him really horny.

But for the purposes of manual sex, the most important thing is that they're neat and clean, so you should err on the side of too short. Just one snagged nail on a super-sensitive frenulum could mean that his trip to paradise turns into a trip to casualty.

The best way to jerk him off is to make your way through all the following techniques, see which one works best for him, and stick with it in a firm movement until he comes, increasing your speed as you sense he's approaching orgasm.

● Make a loose fist with one hand and slide it all the way up the shaft of the penis, twisting with a flourish at the top. Think of it as the Queen's 'royal wave', only upside down. The twist at the end stimulates the head and that's why you should save it for the top. While one hand's at the top twisting, the other one's at the bottom, ready to start it all off again.

● Alternatively, link the fingers of both hands together, almost as though they were clasped loosely in prayer. The effect is a 'one-sided tunnel' formed by the fingers of both hands, with the thumbs completing the circle. The tunnel is then placed over the erect penis, while the hands swivel from side to side so that the whole penis gets the benefit of the tunnel. By moving at the wrist you get a smoother motion than if you were going up and down the penis, and it keeps the tunnel still and steady.

● Run both of your hands in a continuous motion from the top to the bottom of his erection. The key here is not to stop – you want to make him feel like your hands are a never-ending tunnel.

● Don't neglect his balls – cup them with one hand when you're doing the basic up-and-down stroke on the shaft with the other. Tug gently on his testicles and run your fingers lightly along the part of the scrotum that divides them.

● Press firmly on his perineum – the hairless area between his balls and bum – to trip him over the edge of heaven.

● If you're going to play with his anus, warn him first and make sure your fingers are warm and well lubricated.

● Squeeze your breasts together and cradle his penis between them, then shift your way up and down. Or wrap your hair loosely round the shaft of his penis. This last one's more a novelty than anything else – but you won't hear him complaining...

Simultaneous stimulation

Masturbating one another at the same time doesn't often result in simultaneous climax for the simple reason that it's very hard to relax enough to enjoy the sensations you're feeling at your lover's fingertips while concentrating so hard on the work in hand! Some couples overcome this by looking each other in the eye during mutual masturbation, finding that this makes the experience more like lovemaking. Most couples, however, find that taking it in turns to orgasm is less stressful and more successful.

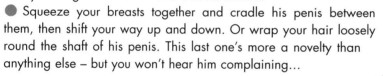

talking dirty

Good sex depends on communication – but words don't always come easy. We expect our partners instinctively to interpret our sex moans and groans – but how is he really meant to know that 'Mmm' means 'I'd like more stimulation on my clitoris, please'? Whether you want to be able to tell your partner what feels good in bed, or you simply want to indulge in some low-down and dirty talking, read on.

The golden rule is to focus on the good rather than the bad – we're never more vulnerable than in bed and a careless word can scar forever. If, for example, your partner doesn't smell as good as they should, don't say: 'I can't have sex with you! You stink!' Instead, remind him of last week when he smelt so sexy fresh out of the shower that you just had to jump his bones there and then on the bathmat. And if you don't like the way your girlfriend uses her teeth too much when she's going down on you, don't tell her it feels like a mangle – next time she's down there, say: 'Mmm, do you know how good you feel when you wrap your lips around your teeth?'

'Tell me how you want me to fuck you.'

A lot of people like dirty talk. It can make sex a lot kinkier and steamier, and some of the things you both shout out in the heat of the moment will clue you in to each other's fantasies and deepest, darkest, dirtiest desires. Dirty talk needs to be introduced gently with a strongly put compliment such as: 'You're the horniest guy I've ever kissed,' or 'You get more sexy every time I fuck you.' See how he reacts to the f-word before you carry on. If your partner needs a bit of encouragement, ask questions that demand an answer more specific than 'yes' or 'no'. Try 'Do you feel good inside me?' or 'Tell me what you want me to do.' And finally – we all shout different things at the moment of orgasm, but you can't go wrong by saying your partner's name. Just make sure it's the right name...

4

getting on down

the Secrets of earth-moving fellatio

There's a famous bloke joke that goes: 'There's no such thing as a bad blow job.' But there is such a thing as excellent oral sex. Perfect these techniques and go down in history as the greatest lover of all times.

Ten steps to heaven for him

1 Run your fingers through his pubic hair before you begin, to stop stray hairs from getting caught in your teeth – the tiny tugging sensations will also turn him on. Cover your lips with your teeth before you go anywhere near his erect penis.

2 'Blow job' is an inaccurate term – it's all about sucking, not blowing. Some men love lots of suction, others prefer you to alternate sucking with lots of little licks and tricks as listed here. Your tongue is very versatile – use it relaxed, wide and flat to arouse him, stroking gently up the shaft and caressing every inch of his penis. For more intense stimulation, flex your tongue so it's narrow and firm, and pay special attention to the more erogenous areas of the penis, such as the veins that run along the underside, and the head. Keep the pressure firm but not too hard – he really is sensitive here. Short, side-to-side licks will 'wake up' a flaccid or flagging penis. Use the underside of your tongue for a wet, textured sensation the

top of your tongue just can't produce. This technique will delight him if you use it on his testicles, because the tiny hairs on his balls can be pulled and snagged by the surface of the top of your tongue. If you're too shy to ask him outright what he likes, put your fingers in his mouth and get him to mimic what he wants you to do to his penis.

3 This is your power trip: it's about you giving pleasure to him, not just lying there while he thrusts in and out of your mouth. Control it by making a ring with your fingers around the base of his penis. This not only stops him thrusting too far, it also creates an extension of your mouth and makes penetration feel deeper for him.

You've got to be in control of the depth and pace.

4 Alternatively, make your thumb and forefinger into an L-shape, so the tiny webbed piece of skin on your hand between the thumb and forefinger is taut. Now use that piece of skin to cradle the underside of his penis while you concentrate on pleasuring the head, and run your tongue along the often-neglected top side of his penis.

5 You will gag at first – but this can be overcome with practice. Rehearse on a sex toy or a cucumber. Push it a few millimetres further down your throat every day for a week and you should be able to accommodate the average penis by the weekend! He loves the feeling of going deep into your mouth because the soft palette and the back of your mouth are in the perfect position to stimulate the head of his penis.

6 Use your hands. Press down on his perineum when he's about to come and watch a grown man weep.

To swallow or not to swallow?

That's the big question – the answer is totally up to you. You shouldn't feel under any pressure either way. If you do swallow, you'll make him feel loved, accepted and welcomed. It's an acquired taste, but try to avoid using words like 'gross' seconds after he's come in your mouth – this will undo all your good work. Keep a glass of water or fruit juice by the bed to refresh your mouth. If you don't want to swallow, there are lots of other sexy options to make semen part of your lovemaking, like asking him to come over your chest, or even in your face, and then massaging it into your skin (be warned: it stings if it gets in your eyes). You should be able to tell when he's about to come by his body language and his moans of delight; but if you're nervous, decide upon a signal which means he's about to come, such as a gentle tug on your hair or ear.

As for what's in it, the main ingredient is the naturally occurring sugar fructose, and there's probably about six calories in the average ejaculate, so you don't need to worry it'll make you fat. Feed him the right foods to improve the taste of his semen – keep the fridge stocked with fruit, and avoid spicy foods, tobacco, alcohol, coffee and red meat.

7 If you need a break, move his penis from the middle of your mouth to your cheek.

8 Don't keep his penis in your mouth throughout. Withdraw until he's outside and then bear down on him again. Closing your lips lightly before taking him in feels a lot like vaginal penetration and pays special attention to the tip of his penis, which is the most sensitive part. Make sure he can see his penis as it slides in and out of your mouth.

9 Ball games are allowed. Run your tongue over his testicles and take them into your mouth, one at a time. Drive him wild by gently humming while you've got one of his balls between your lips.

10 Look him in the eye and let him know you're enjoying it.

Positions

● The most popular position for fellatio is to have him lie back on a bed or sofa while you sit or kneel between his legs. This way you can look up at him sexily, use your breasts to caress his balls, kiss up and down his body and take as long as you want. You can reach

up and pinch his nipples and caress his buttocks. You'll be doing a lot of work, moving the whole of your body, but it's your gift to him, and he'll feel utterly pampered.

● Another position to try is with him standing up and you kneeling at his feet. This is a huge male fantasy because it makes him feel all-powerful: you might be in mild discomfort, but you're being utterly subservient to his desires, which is a major turn-on. In this position, the back of your throat will keep his penis feeling nice and snug, and you're in a great place to use the back of your tongue on the head of his penis. He'll feel like he's got control because he can thrust a bit, and you'll love it because, as you fix him with a sexy stare from down there on your knees, you know the power is all yours!

● He lies or crouches over you on all fours and places his penis in your mouth. Think of it as an oral sex missionary position. He'll enjoy it because he has a good degree of control over the depth and penetration, and it can be good for you as you have to do very little but lie there. You will, however, need to be very relaxed in order to accommodate him – and you'll need your head propped up on pillows so he can reach you.

the Secrets of spine-tingling Cunnilingus

The one thing men and women alike report wanting more of in bed is oral sex. Cunnilingus, going down on her, licking her out – whatever you call it, done right, it's virtually guaranteed to give her an orgasm. Here's how.

Ten steps to heaven for her

1 Women enjoy oral sex because it's soft and wet and, unlike vigorous intercourse, it doesn't leave them feeling sore. So don't think of your tongue as a mini penis – you may thrust in and out of the vagina, but the best results come from concentrating on the clitoris.

2 Start by kissing her labia the same way you'd kiss the lips on her face.

3 Smother the clitoris with your tongue to begin with, rather than flicking it. Draw letters on her clitoris, and circle around it first before going for the bud.

4 Use your hands too. Caress her breasts, run your fingers through her pubic hair, stroke her clitoris, buttocks and inner thighs.

5 To create a more taut, accessible surface for your tongue, expose more sensitive skin and make the clitoris easier to find, hold the top of her labia open with one hand. Or ask her to do it so your hands are free to caress her.

6 It's crucial to maintain a slow, steady rhythm. If she says she likes what you're doing, that means keep on doing *exactly* what you're doing, not step up the pace.

7 Use your whole face – a nose nuzzled in the top of her vulva while your tongue is thrusting inside will give her vaginal and clitoral stimulation. Make sure, however, that you shave properly beforehand; otherwise you'll be all scratchy. Moisturise your skin, too, and if you've got a beard, use hair conditioner on it.

8 Orgasm can take a while, especially if this is the first part of foreplay. Be patient and don't try to rush things: the slower you go, the faster she'll get there.

9 Use the top and bottom of your tongue: they produce very different sensations.

10 Let her know how much you enjoyed the experience.

Positions

● The classic cunnilingus position entails your partner lying back on the edge of a bed or chair with you between her legs. It's marvellous for her because all she has to do is lie back and enjoy; she also has quite a degree of control because she can spread and tighten her legs and move her hips to guide you. Most women are more sensitive to stimulation on one side of the clitoris – if her legs are spread wide apart like this, you can explore with your tongue until you find her own particular hot spot. You'll find it much easier to keep up the steady rhythm needed if you support your neck with a pillow. If she throws her leg over your shoulder, it makes it easier for her to rock in time with your rhythm, and is also a great opportunity for you to penetrate her with your tongue.

● Ask her to sit on your face. Slip a pillow under your head, if necessary, and lie still while she gyrates over your lips, tongue and nose (never underestimate the effect of a well-placed nose nudge). Use both upward and downward motions and lots of suction. She can be facing either way – facing you is best for clitoral stimulation, while away from you lets you play with her anus and perineum. As great as this feels, she may not be able to relax, and it does require a lot of

Natural sex appeal

Many women say they're unable to enjoy oral sex because they're concerned about their personal hygiene; they worry that their partners will be turned off if their vaginas don't smell shower-fresh at all times. Well, here's the good news: the natural musky smell you give off is packed with pheromones and is a powerful aphrodisiac, so much so that the French call the female genital scent the cassolette, meaning little perfume box. Showering once or twice a day and using a mild soap should keep you as fresh as you need to be: constantly deodorising yourself with douches and scented products could actually damage the delicate pH balance of your vagina and do more harm than good. If you're genuinely worried about a bad smell coming from down there, see your GP – it could be a sign of an infection.

Lots of things can affect the way you taste. To keep yourself as sweet as possible, stick to a light, vegetarian diet, and be aware that you might not taste so nice after drinking coffee or alcohol or smoking cigarettes. There's also the issue of pubic hair. Some men love natural bushiness while others go wild at the sight of a shaven haven – for oral sex, short is sweet. Not only will your skin be more sensitive if you crop your pubic hair, but he'll be keener to go down on you if there's less risk of stray hairs getting caught between his teeth.

thigh power not to crush you. She may find it more comfortable to lean forward on the bed. If you don't think you can go the distance, use this position as a prelude to the classic cunnilingus position above.

● Do it with her standing up if you want a quickie. This is quite literally a knee-trembler, and can be very sexy if you're at a formal party where she's wearing a long gown. You'll have to squat or kneel down in order to kiss her. Use upward motions along the labia and fast, darting motions on the clitoris. You might get a crick in your neck, but the thrill of this position could mean she comes more quickly.

● Hold her upside down: she lies back on the floor while you kneel down on the edge of the bed or sofa, bending forwards, with her legs over your shoulders. The view from your end will be arousing, and you can maintain eye contact throughout. This will also make the blood rush to her head – as if the orgasmic sensations weren't making her feel deliciously dizzy enough…

advanced Oral

Once you've mastered the basic techniques of fellatio and cunnilingus, you might want to experiment with '69', deep throat and other oral sex tricks for adventurous lovers!

The 69er

This got its name because the numbers are head to toe, just as you are. It means both of you giving each other oral sex at the same time. It's the *idea* of simultaneous oral sex that's the big turn-on – in practice, it's not easy to give and receive pleasure at the same time. So don't worry if you don't see stars the first time you try it.

The 69 position is great for those times when you're feeling fun and frisky and orgasm isn't the immediate goal, or save it for occasions when you're both so horny that the lightest touch will bring you to orgasm. The best way to perform the 69 is to take it in turns: spend alternate minutes stimulating one another's genitals – this should build up to a tremendous orgasm for both of you. Or use it as foreplay and savour what you've just done while you're making love.

Her on top This is the most common 69 position for the simple reason that women tend to be lighter than men. He lies flat on his back, with his arms by his sides or around her buttocks. She's on all fours with her bottom in the air, hovering over his face. She rests on her forearms. Her mouth is poised over his penis. The benefits of this position are that she can control the rhythm of the cunnilingus she's receiving by rocking her hips in time, and she's perfectly positioned to pay attention to every inch of his penis. Her breasts will brush against his belly and thighs, which will turn him on and the friction on her nipples will stimulate her, too. His arms are free to caress her or to stimulate himself if she gets tired. And of course, from his point of view, there's less work for his pleasure!

Him on top He crouches over her on all fours and is in an excellent position to play with her breasts – he can see exactly what he's doing, which makes him more likely to hit the right spot. This is a comfortable position for him because his neck won't start to ache – he can also use her inner thighs for a pillow. He uses a downward motion on her labia and clitoris. It's not easy for the woman to take him fully into her mouth from this angle, but he can thrust against her neck, cheeks and breasts and she's free to use her tongue on his anus, balls and perineum.

Deep throat

Not everyone can pull off this porn-film favourite; it requires a very relaxed palate, but the result will be a very grateful penis. Lie back with your head hanging off the edge of the bed and your mouth open. He kneels or stands at the edge of the bed, depending on how high you are. It might be easier for you if he's kneeling, as standing up he's able to thrust harder than you might like. The idea is to create as long a passage as possible to accommodate his penis. If he's thrusting too hard and you feel choked, stop and resume oral sex in a more comfortable position.

Rimming

Also known as analingus, rimming is the fine art of using the tongue to stimulate the anus. It's been a well-kept secret of gay sex for years, but can be enjoyed by men and women alike. This shouldn't be attempted unless the recipient is fresh from the shower, and should be avoided if the giver has any open cuts on or around the mouth, as this part of the body is particularly vulnerable to infection. Move the tongue in tiny, circular movements around the thin skin of the anus – imagine you're using your tongue to trace an image of the curly wire of a telephone cord.

Mouthwatering treats
If your oral sex sessions are getting a bit tired, the following surprises will help to spice up the experience:

● Put toothpaste on his balls for an ever-increasing heat sensation – blow on them to tease him.

● Place crushed ice in her vagina to numb it slightly – the sensations for both of you will be amazing. This one's fun to try on a sunny holiday.

● Dribble a little champagne into her vagina and then drink from her.

● Give him a blow job just after you've been sipping a cup of hot tea or sucking on an ice cube – or, for the ultimate experience, alternate the two!

● Clean your tongue with a toothbrush beforehand. A healthy pink tongue is a real turn-on.

● Lick your lips before you start.

● Go down on your partner wearing a slick of medicated or menthol lip balm – he or she will enjoy that medicated tingle below the belt…

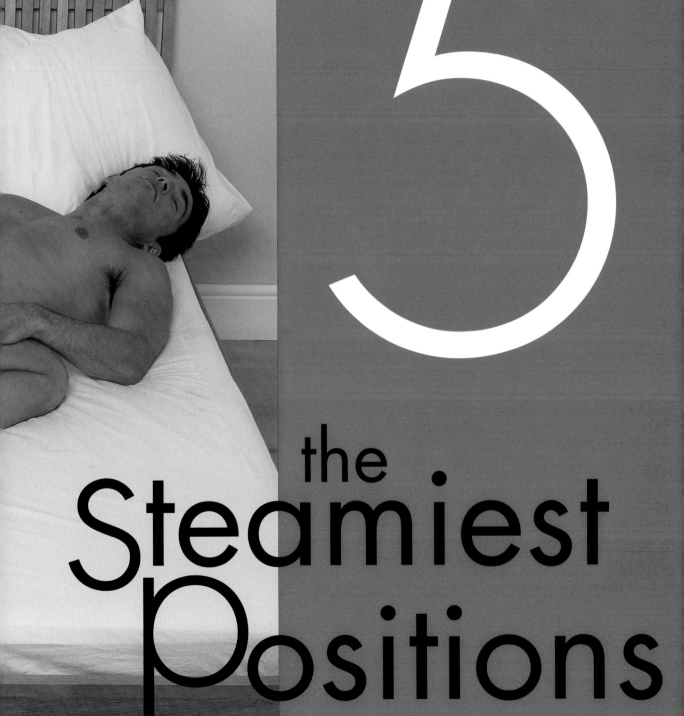

5

the
Steamiest
positions

Woman on top

Girl power! Sex is adventurous and orgasmic when women take the lead in bed. These positions are great for women who like to be in control – and he'll love it when you show off your body and let him lie back and relax for a change.

The rodeo

How to do it He lies on his back; he may find it more comfortable with his head propped up on pillows or resting in his cradled hands. She straddles him and gently slides herself down onto his erection and uses her thighs to move up and down.

What's right with it? It's great for the guy because all he has to do is lie back and enjoy the experience – watching her breasts bounce up and down is a huge visual treat for him. Both partners have access to her breasts and clitoris and he can use his hands to guide her hips into the rhythm he likes. This is a great position during pregnancy as her 'bump' won't be squashed.

What's wrong with it? Unless she has the thighs of a horse-riding champion, this position can get very tiring very quickly, and

can induce cramp. What's more, some women say that it makes them feel too exposed. The position can be frustrating for the man who likes to control the thrusting during sex, although he can grab hold of her buttocks or her waist to help her move up and down.

Variations on the theme This is a great opportunity to wear sexy lingerie or to show off a fantasy outfit during sex: why not try a chiffon and marabou nightie or a see-through negligée?

Reverse rodeo

How to do it He lies back and she squats over him, facing his feet, and slowly lowers herself onto his erection. She leans on her hands and bounces up and down or, if she wants to show off how flexible she is, she can lean back over his chest so that they are lying cheek-to-cheek.

What's right with it? There's not much work in here for the man. When she's sitting up, he's free to stimulate her anus and perineum if that's what she likes; and if she's lying back, he can reach her clitoris. Because you can't see each other, you're free to let your fantasies run wild. It's the only way to combine the thrill of rear-entry sex with the snug fit of woman-on-top sex.

What's wrong with it? It can take a while to find a position with which both partners are comfortable and offers little clitoral stimulation for her through intercourse alone; what's more, as he can't reach her clitoris, she'll have to stimulate it herself.

Variations on the theme She could start by sitting on his face to give her arousal a head start and then work her way down his body.

X-factor

How to do it He lies back on pillows with his legs apart, while she lowers herself onto his penis and slowly, slowly, shifts back until she's lying backwards at a similar angle to him, with her legs extended. From the side, the two of you should look like the letter X.

What's right with it? You've got great eye contact and can see the penis sliding in and out of the vagina, which is a big turn-on. Penetration feels unusual, especially at the tip of his dick, and because there's little range of movement, the man's orgasm can be delayed. This is great if either of you is particularly heavy or become claustrophobic during body-contact sex – you both have a real sense of your own space as you're joined at the hip and nowhere else.

What's wrong with it? Gently does it with this position: the penis is at an unusual and precarious angle. Pull out too quickly and you'll know about it for the wrong reasons. Because of the delicate nature of the position, you're going to have to take it slow.

Variations on the theme If you've got access to a bedroom with a mirrored ceiling you'll find the view from above highly erotic.

Scissors

How to do it He lies back and she squats over him, facing his feet, and slowly lowers herself onto his erection. She then leans forward and extends her legs behind her, and slowly rocks up and down on his penis.

What's right with it? Her full weight is bearing down on his penis, creating an incredibly snug fit. She can squeeze his penis with her buttocks during intercourse to make penetration feel even deeper, and can grab onto his legs as she thrusts to help her balance. The more she shifts around, the more different parts of the penis and vagina can be stimulated. If she's worried about putting too much weight on him, she can lean into his thighs.

What's wrong with it? She can't lie still because the angle of her vagina around his penis would be too uncomfortable for him. And if she's not confident about the way her bottom looks, this isn't the position for her!

Variations on the theme If he's got a foot fetish, this is the perfect position in which to indulge it – he can suck on her toes during their lovemaking.

The hooker

How to do it He sits up on the bed with his legs slightly bent. She lowers herself onto his erection, wraps her arms around his neck to balance and hooks both of her legs over his shoulders. Orgasm is reached by a slow, rocking motion.

What's right with it? This position is very intimate: you're quite literally wrapped up in each other and it's easy to talk and kiss throughout. It also combines deep penetration with access to her clitoris, increasing her chances of simultaneous vaginal and clitoral orgasm. As you can't move very much, it's slow, gentle and sensual.

What's wrong with it? Balancing isn't easy – if you find it hard, try it with him leaning back against the headboard. She'll need to be quite supple to keep her legs in place throughout intercourse. And if you like to thrust vigorously, there's little room to do that here.

Variations on the theme Sex in this position is even steamier if she keeps her stockings and suspenders on throughout – he can kiss and stroke her sexy legs during intercourse.

Female missionary

How to do it He lies back while she climbs on top of him, facing forwards, supporting her weight on her forearms and extending her legs behind her. She moves her whole body up and down to massage his penis. She can press her legs together to increase clitoral stimulation, or spread them wide for deeper penetration.

What's right with it? This is one of the only woman-on-top positions where you're close enough to kiss and talk throughout, which creates intimacy. Both of you can enjoy full-body, skin-on-skin contact, and sensitive areas like the breasts are naturally stimulated, while his pubic bone rubs against her clitoris. Stopping the motion for a second to bend down and kiss can delay his orgasm: lovely if you want to keep him from coming too soon.

What's wrong with it? Although some men love it when women take the lead like this, it can be frustrating not to be able to control the depth and speed of penetration. And if there's a big difference in your heights, this doesn't work.

Variations on the theme This is a fantastic position for him to enjoy if he likes to be restrained during sex. Cuff him to the bedpost, tie his legs down and have your wicked way with him!

man on top

Whoever said man-on-top sex was traditional and boring obviously hasn't tried these highly erotic twists. The following positions are designed to bring out the masculine and feminine qualities in each of you during lovemaking, and are powerful and passionate.

Missionary

How to do it She lies on her back with her legs parted. He lies over her, supporting his weight on his elbows, enters her, and thrusts.

What's right with it? This isn't the most popular lovemaking position for nothing: it's powerfully erotic, with the woman at her most open and vulnerable and the man able to exercise his full sexual power. He controls most of the thrusting and there's very little effort involved for her. Kissing and talking is possible throughout, as is all-important eye contact. There's close body contact too.

What's wrong with it? It offers little for the woman who wants to take the lead, and it can be hard to maintain clitoral stimulation.

Variations on the theme The chances of her reaching orgasm are much greater if she places a pillow under her hips. This alters the entire tilt of her pelvis, exposing her clitoris to much more friction.

The tie-me-up tango

How to do it From a kneeling position, she lies on her back with her legs folded under her thighs so her pelvis is elevated. She flings her arms above her head while he lies on top of her.

What's right with it? This enables really deep thrusting, and his hands are free to explore erogenous zones that aren't always accessible during intercourse, such as her underarms and sides. Her breasts will also be sensitive to stimulation because they're stretched taut, exposing each nerve ending to his touch. This is an excellent position for lesbian lovemaking, with or without a strap-on, because the friction of two sets of breasts brushing against each other is hugely arousing.

What's wrong with it? She has to be quite flexible to maintain this position for the entire lovemaking session; her knees and thigh muscles may get quite tired. Also, she can't use her hands to control his hips by thrusting, nor can she stimulate his or her genitals. But that helplessness is part of the attraction here.

Variations on the theme Blindfold her to make her surrender even more complete.

The tabletop

How to do it She lies on a flat surface like a table with her legs in the air. He leans against her legs, supporting her and holding her feet together, while he penetrates her.

What's right with it? Great for when you want to take sex out of the bedroom – this is fab for the kitchen table, your desk at work or the car bonnet. The angle of her vagina in this position stimulates every nerve ending in his penis, from the sensitive head to the shaft. This is also the best man-on-top position for hitting her G-spot. Clitoral stimulation is possible and she can play with her breasts to great effect as she lies on her back.

What's wrong with it? She might feel a bit vulnerable, and he has to make sure he's holding her at all times so she doesn't go flying off the table – which might put him off his stroke.

Variations on the theme She wears thigh-high leather boots with spiky heels that dig into his shoulders, nearly crossing the fine line between pleasure and pain.

The flower press

How to do it He kneels on the bed and she lies back and brings her knees right up to her chin, so that when he enters her, her feet are at either side of his head or resting on his chest. He holds onto her thighs or shins, and she grabs onto his hips.

What's right with it? Her pelvis really tilts up, allowing for perhaps the deepest penetration possible in a man-on-top position. If he likes feet, this is great. Because the two bodies aren't squashed together her breasts and clitoris can be stimulated. She can also slide her legs in between his legs and gently tug on his balls or press his perineum.

What's wrong with it? There's not much scope for kissing. Sometimes he can get carried away with the thrusting because it's so deep, but it's a great position for men with little dicks.

Variations on the theme Lock her feet around his head by placing her ankles in a pair of leg restraints.

Missionary, legs inside

How to do it She lies on her back and spreads her legs so he can penetrate her. Once he's inside, instead of wrapping her legs around his calves, she slides them down onto the bed so they're straight and resting just inside his thighs.

What's right with it? By squeezing her legs together, she can make her vagina feel longer and snugger, which is useful for accommodating a man with an extremely large penis. The odd super squeeze of her thighs will also stimulate her clitoris and give her a stronger orgasm; if she wants to regain a bit of control she can use her hands to push his buttocks deeper in. She can squeeze him with her pubococcygeal muscle (see page 15).

What's wrong with it? She can't move very much.

Variations on the theme If she gets off on the idea of helplessness, pin her arms down by her sides or strap her to the bed using body wrap or a leather harness.

Wraparound

How to do it She lies on her back, with her arms and legs wide open. He crouches over her on all fours and penetrates her; she wraps her arms and legs around his shoulders and back to maintain penetration – she may want to prop her back and pelvis up on pillows to make it more comfortable.

What's right with it? She can use her legs to force his thighs and buttocks, driving him deeper in. Lots of movement, rocking and thrusting is possible; the constant shifting of positions and angles ensures that his penis receives top-to-toe stimulation – and there's a greater chance than normal of her G-spot being caressed by the tip of his penis. Homosexual male couples can enjoy this position as part of foreplay, kissing and rubbing against each other, or turn it into the main event – the rubbing together of two erect penises, known as 'frottage', can produce an orgasm in itself.

What's wrong with it? Opportunities for mutual masturbation and stimulation are limited. He may feel that her arms and legs prevent him from thrusting as much as he wants to. He also needs a pretty strong back as it's supporting much of her bodyweight.

Variations on the theme If you enjoy anal play, having sex in this position using butt-plugs or Thai beads (see page 153) will drive you wild.

The woman has more participation and control in Wraparound than is usual during missionary position intercourse.

Side by Side

Sex in this position is perfect when you want your lovemaking to be slow and sensuous. Many couples enjoy making love side by side as both partners feel equal – neither of you is on top and you share control of pace and penetration. The following positions also require very little effort!

Face to face

How to do it The simplest way to reach this position is to roll over on to your sides from a man-on-top position, sustaining penetration as you go. To start from scratch, she will need to lie on her side and part her legs so that he can penetrate her.

What's right with it? You can speak, kiss and caress – in fact, you need to keep cuddling throughout as, if you let go suddenly, you might fall backwards and apart. The shallow penetration of this position means its great if he's got an oversized penis.

What's wrong with it? If you like lots of thrusting, rhythmical sex you'll find this side-by-side position too gentle for you. You also run the risk of squashing each other's thighs.

Variations on the theme Cover yourselves in massage oil and slip-slide all over a rubber sheet to make this position even more exciting.

Spoons

How to do it She lies on her side while he snuggles up behind her. She then draws up her knees a bit and opens her thighs while he tucks his knees behind her, entering her from the rear.

What's right with it? Sweet and slow, spoons sex is great for sex at the end of the day when you're both feeling lazy. You don't even have to change positions to fall asleep in each other's arms. This is also a chance to really indulge the super-sensitive erogenous zones around the neck, ears and shoulders, whether that's with a massage or nuzzling and kissing. No position better lends itself to him whispering sweet nothings in her ear.

What's wrong with it? If his penis is small, or one of you is overweight and you can't snuggle as closely as you'd like, penetration can feel a little too shallow for both of you.

Variations on the theme Cuff your legs together to bring a thrilling, dangerous element of bondage into an otherwise safe and intimate position.

The back flip

How to do it An advanced version of the spoons position, he lies on his back and penetrates her from behind while she's snuggled on top of his body, facing away from him.

What's right with it? He's got great access to her breasts and clitoris and this position will make him feel incredibly masculine as he thrusts, supporting her weight. It's also a good position for her if she finds it easier to climax when they're not face-to-face. When she does orgasm, he'll feel the contractions of her anus and perineum because his penis is close to the back wall of her vagina. If she's much taller or lighter than him, this position is ideal.

The man can thrust for a long time in the Back Flip position, as penetration isn't particularly deep.

What's wrong with it? If she's heavy, neither partner will have much scope for movement and they won't be able to thrust very much – he might need both of his hands for balancing as well. Also, it's not recommended for couples with back problems – physical fitness is an advantage!

Variations on the theme If you're a fan of alfresco sex, this position allows you to soak up the sun on your skin while you sin!

The 'Y'

How to do it She lies on her side facing him, with one leg in the air and the other on the bed, propping herself up on one arm – her body should look like a huge 'Y' shape. He straddles the lower leg while the lifted leg rests on his shoulder and he penetrates her from the side.

What's right with it? You both have a great view of each other's face and body. He can see his penis sliding in and out of her vagina and has a clear view of her anus. He can also stimulate her inner thighs. As her legs are so well spread, he can thrust however he wants – from short, sharp strokes to slow, powerful pumps.

What's wrong with it? Balancing can be tricky – it can also be difficult for him to establish a steady rhythm.

Variations on the theme This makes a great one to video – especially with a handheld camcorder.

Sitting down

Ladies and gentlemen, please take your seats for these intimate sex positions. Sitting down lends itself to a variety of outrageous occasions – and if you make it a regular part of your lovemaking routine, you'll have the strong, toned thighs of a ski instructor.

Two turtle doves

How to do it The couple sit facing each other, with their legs crossed or wrapped around each other's backs. They then inch together until he's penetrating her and slowly rock their way to orgasm, scratching each other's backs and massaging each other's fronts all the way through.

What's right with it? She's bearing down on his penis with all her weight, making for deep and massaging penetration. Being on top, she calls the shots on the pace and depth; he doesn't have to do very much. Because her legs are spread, the skin around her clitoris is stretched thinner and is even more sensitive to his touch. It's also easy for the couple to kiss. This is a great position for lesbians using a double dildo or vibrators on each other.

What's wrong with it? It can be hard to balance, so don't let go of each other. The man may feel frustrated if she doesn't thrust as hard or as deep as he likes.

Variations on the theme She can reach between his legs – a well-timed squeeze on the scrotum can send him over the edge.

Lap dance

How to do it He sits on a chair with his legs together. She sits on his lap, and lowers herself backwards onto his penis. Orgasm is achieved through rocking and thrusting.

What's right with it? His penis is at a great angle to stimulate her G-spot and they can both reach forwards to play with her clitoris or breasts. The lap dance is fun, but if you prefer positions with a greater range of movement, it's very easy to move from this position, without him having to pull out, into the doggy style or another pose that lets you shake it all about!

What's wrong with it? Success depends on her moving her thighs to control the depth and the thrust of penetration, which can get quite tiring for her.

Variations on the theme Both of you are looking in the same direction, so this position is great if you're both looking at something that turns you on – try it on the sofa in front of a dirty video, or in front of a full-length mirror.

Sitting pretty

How to do it He sits in a sturdy chair while she straddles him, her knees up, either side of his chest. Holding onto the back of the chair, she pushes away with her feet and moves up and down on his penis while he caresses her.

What's right with it? This is a fantastic position for quickie sex, as well as being fun and intimate. Her breasts are in a great position for him to take into his mouth while she bounces up and down. He can control the speed of her movements by placing his hands on her waist and gently guiding her.

What's wrong with it? As she bears down, her bodyweight can feel heavy on his thighs, which can put him off. And she might be concentrating so hard on moving up and down that she can't relax enough to orgasm.

Variations on the theme For ultimate stimulation, she can use her thighs to raise herself up so that only the tip of his penis is inside her vagina. Using her PC muscles to make sure he doesn't fall out, she can then gently swivel her hips from side to side before slowly sliding back down again so that the whole length of his penis is inside her once more.

Standing Up

For urgent, passionate, got-to-have-you-now lovemaking, you can't beat sex standing up. It's demanding and passion-packed, and not for everyday intercourse – but what a treat for a special occasion!

The quickie

How to do it This is the perfect position for those moments when you just can't wait to get to the bedroom, and is designed for maximum orgasms in minimum time. She sits on a surface about the same height as his pelvis and wraps her legs around his back. If there's no available kitchen worktop or desk, you can make love up against the wall, but this offers less support for both of you. She pulls her skirt up and pushes her panties to one side while he unzips his flies or drops his trousers.

What's right with it? The thrill of having a quickie can speed up the female sexual response, meaning she comes in a fraction of the time she would normally take. Her weight is supported by the worktop so all her energy can be put into her sexual performance rather than standing up straight! This also gives him more scope to thrust.

You don't even need to get totally undressed for this classic, coming-in-a jiffy position.

What's wrong with it? Sometimes women can't produce enough lubrication in time for quickie sex, no matter how turned on they are. Carry a phial of lube with you to avoid this problem.

Variations on the theme Keeping your clothes on is practical as well as sexy. Wear clothes that can easily be pulled to one side rather than whipped off.

Carry on

How to do it He begins on his knees and asks her to lower herself onto his erection, facing him. As she does, she wraps her legs around his waist and puts her arms around his neck. Then he slowly stands up, shaking her up and down.

What's right with it? This position reinforces ideas of masculinity and femininity, which will make you both feel sexy. If the two of you can last until you're ready to orgasm, the sensations will be amazing. There's enough full-body contact and friction between you to turn both of you on and speed orgasm along.

What's wrong with it? It helps if he's very strong – and won't work at all if she's too heavy for him. If you can't handle more than a minute in this position, incorporate it into your foreplay routine or find a surface on which she can balance her feet, such as the edge of the bed or a kitchen worktop.

Variations on the theme Use a gag so no-one can hear your moans of delight!

Stairway to heaven

How to do it She stands on the stair in front of him, facing away from him, and he enters her from behind. Once penetration is established, he circles one arm around her stomach and grabs hold of her leg with the other. She then carefully lifts her legs behind her so he's supporting her.

What's right with it? This ambitious position is great if you're pretending to star in a porn movie – or indeed, if you're actually filming yourselves. It's exhibitionist, sexy and fun. She'll love the feeling of total sexual surrender while he feels dominant and masculine.

What's wrong with it? It's incredibly physically demanding: he needs to be pretty strong, and she needs to be flexible. Balancing is hard for both of you, and you'll both tire easily. Get around this by indulging in lots of mutual foreplay first, so that you're both on the brink of orgasm before intercourse takes place.

Variations on the theme If fatigue takes over, she can lean forward and place her hands on the floor. This still offers the deep penetration and naughtiness that's the appeal of the Stairway to Heaven, but is a lot less stressful for both of you!

Sexplosion
positions for the most powerful orgasms

Want the kind of sex you see in the movies? The kind of sex where women have multiple orgasms and both of you come at the same time? The good news is that this dream is entirely possible with these advanced techniques. They take a while to master, but once you've got the hang of them, they'll become your new favourite positions!

The cat

How to do it Coming together is totally achievable with this incredible position. Short for the Coital Alignment Technique, the cat is a new approach to intercourse based on pressure and rocking motions rather than thrusting. He gets on top of her, lining his pelvis up over hers. His penis is inside, but he's riding high so the base of his penis is just outside her vagina, and his pubic bone is pressing down on her pubic hair. She wraps her legs around his thighs and rests her ankles on his calves. They then move just their pelvises, not their arms or legs, at the same speed, pushing up and down against each other. The aim is to move in the same way at the same speed.

What's right with it? Not only are women three times more likely to experience orgasm through this technique, but also it delays the male orgasm so your chances of coming together are greater.

What's wrong with it? The technique is not an easy one to master because it depends on the rocking and rolling mechanism rather than thrusting, which is the way we all learn how to have sex. It does take patience, and can be uncomfortable if she's much smaller than him.

Variations on the theme Play a slow, sexy song that turns both of you on and see if you can keep time to the music.

Come again

How to do it This is the best position for women to achieve multiple orgasms. He lies back while she lowers herself onto him. Then she draws her legs up so her knees are parallel with her chest, and shifts her pelvis so that her clitoris is directly over his pubic bone. Orgasm is reached by gently rocking over him. He should hold off orgasm until hers has been achieved. Then, if she's able to climax again, penetration can continue. If not, she can help him orgasm by masturbating him or performing fellatio.

What's right with it? This position combines the three factors most likely to contribute to female orgasm: full body contact, clitoral attention and varying degrees of vaginal stimulation. She controls the position of her pelvis so she can be sure that her clitoris is aligned with his pubic bone, and because he can't thrust, she can manipulate the movements to suit her needs. By drawing her legs up towards her chest, she can alter the angle and depth of her vagina, making it much more likely that his penis will stimulate her G-spot.

What's wrong with it? If the woman wants a multiple orgasm she's going to have to work quite hard for it, and this takes practice and patience to master. But the end will justify the means!

Variations on the theme For a mind-blowing climax for both of you, use a sex toy that combines a cock ring with a clitoral vibrator.

rearentry

If it's deep penetration and G-spot stimulation you're after, rear-entry sex does it every time. This kind of sex tends to be fast and furious, as many people find it so arousing that they can't contain their climax for more than a couple of minutes. Because the position of the female G-spot isn't the same in every woman, try a few variations on the theme to see what works for you.

The doggy

How to do it She kneels on all fours, her legs slightly parted. He kneels up behind her and penetrates her vagina from behind, holding onto her hips, and thrusts.

What's right with it? This is the most common rear-entry sex position for lots of good reasons. The angle of penetration means that his penis is in prime position to caress her G-spot, which is located on the front wall of her vagina. For women who know for sure they have a G-spot, this is a firm favourite. For women who aren't sure, this is a fun way to find out – and there's always the option of stroking her own clitoris while he thrusts. Although he ultimately controls penetration, she can move in time with his rhythm, bearing down and backwards on his penis to make the penetration – which is already deep – even more intense. He can enjoy watching his penis enter her vagina.

What's wrong with it? If his penis is very large, this position can be a little overwhelming. Some women also find it too impersonal and animalistic. Because it's such an intense buzz, many men experience premature ejaculation in this position.

Variations on the theme This position is great for dirty talk – play animal games by putting her on a collar and lead and listen to her yelp with pleasure.

Layers

She lies on her front and raises her behind towards him, spreading her legs to make penetration easier for him. He lies on top of her, resting his weight on his elbows, takes her from behind and thrusts backwards and forwards.

What's right with it? This is great for the man who enjoys being in total control during sex – she can barely move and he's in charge of the depth and pace. By the same token, it's a real turn-on for the woman who loves to surrender during lovemaking. Penetration is snug for him and stimulates her G-spot. Even better, the friction he's causing should mean that her clitoris rubs deliciously against the bedclothes. He can also plant sexy kisses on erogenous zones such as her ears and neck.

What's wrong with it? If she's top heavy, this might get uncomfortable for her, so slip a pillow or a folded-up towel under her midriff. It's also hard for her to access her clitoris manually.

Because you can't see each other, this position is a great one for indulging your fantasies.

Variations on the theme This is a great position in which to play spanking games, using a hand, the back of a hairbrush or a custom-made paddle. For more on sex toys, turn to pages 149–55.

Head rush

How to do it She lies on her back, her hands propping her weight up as though she's about to do a shoulderstand. He kneels before her and pulls her ankles up towards his shoulders, so her legs are resting on his body and her ankles are around his neck.

What's right with it? The upside-down position makes the blood rush to her head, which leads to an all-over tingly orgasm. He controls the penetration. The unusual view for both partners means the novelty is thrilling. He can also access her clitoris if he's brave enough to let go of her legs for a second.

What's wrong with it? The position requires suppleness and stamina on the part of both of you. Penetration can be difficult if you're not used to this position.

Variations on the theme She shaves her pubic hair to make his view even more arousing – or he can shave it for her as a part of their foreplay.

Standing doggy

How to do it He needs a full erection before attempting this position. She stands leaning against a wall or holding onto something for support. He gets behind her and bends his legs until he's low enough to penetrate her from the rear. You'll both have an even greater range of movement if she bends down during this one – she can hold onto his ankles to help her balance.

What's right with it? It's urgent, animalistic and energetic. Her closed legs act as an extension of the vagina, making for tighter penetration for him and stimulating the nerve endings on her labia and inner thighs. It's great if you like the idea of anal sex but don't want to try it, as it's an unusual sensation and you can't really see what's going on, so you're free to fantasise.

What's wrong with it? It might be a little too energetic for some. It also doesn't work if there's a big discrepancy in height. This position is perfect, however, for lesbians of about the same height, wearing a strap-on.

Variations on the theme
She keeps her fingernails long so she can leave little crescent-shaped imprints when she grabs on to his buttocks, begging to have him deeper inside her.

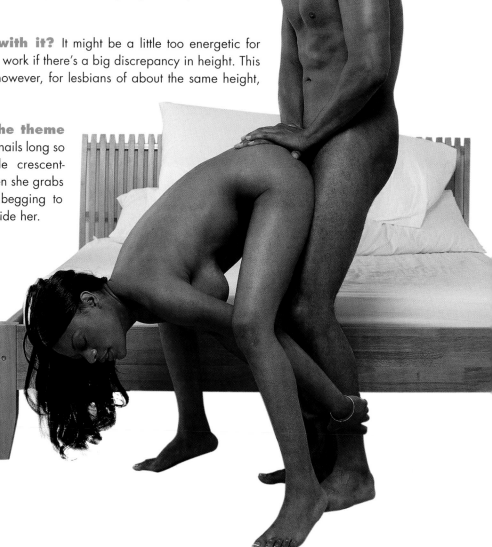

anal Sex

The positions here can be incorporated into either heterosexual or homosexual lovemaking. Homosexual men enjoy anal sex because the prostate gland (which nestles a couple of centimetres or so up the front wall of the rectum) is stimulated, occasionally to the point of orgasm. Women who enjoy anal sex say they like the unusual depth and snugness it provides. Whether you're a girl–boy couple, a boy–boy couple or even a girl–girl couple using a strap-on, the rules are the same for anal sex: you should always use lubricant, because unlike the vagina, the anus doesn't produce its own natural juices. And, even if you've both been given a clean bill of sexual health, you should always use extra-strong condoms, as anal sex makes both of you more vulnerable to infection.

The right angle

How to do it She leans forward, with her upper body at a right angle to her legs. She supports herself by leaning on a surface, while her partner stands behind and penetrates her from the rear, holding on to her thighs.

What's right with it? Because her anus is stretched and exposed in this position, penetration is easy and quick. The angle of her rectum also means that penetration is deep and satisfying. Because she's leaning on something, thrusting is easy for him, and so is balancing.

What's wrong with it? It can feel a little impersonal and out of control for the recipient. Also, penetration is sometimes so deep that the penetrating partner can get a little carried away.

Variations on the theme Lean over a sturdy banister at the top of your stairs for an even giddier sensation.

Bedrock

How to do it She lies with her back on the edge of the bed and her legs raised. She may need to put a pillow or two under her pelvis for ease of access. He stands on the floor and penetrates her, grabbing onto her legs or thighs, if necessary, to balance.

What's right with it? Partners can maintain eye contact throughout intercourse, and she can vary the degree of penetration by putting her legs up on his chest to make it deeper, or wrap her legs around his back to increase the feeling of intimacy and involvement. This position offers a good opportunity for vaginal and clitoral stimulation as well.

What's wrong with it? The thrusting is a lot of work for him, and she can feel as though the lovemaking is out of her control.

Variations on the theme Great for couples into SM and bondage: she can whip him on the buttocks during intercourse with a cat-o'-nine-tails.

There are many surprising and delicious sensations to be had in this position.

The snake

How to do it She lies on her stomach and spreads her legs while he penetrates her from behind, supporting his bodyweight on his arms. She might need to put a pillow or a cushion under her hips to facilitate penetration.

> **The sexy, sweaty skin-on-skin contact releases pheromones that up the ante for both of you.**

What's right with it? Penetration is shallow, so it's ideal if he's got a particularly big penis that she can't accommodate comfortably. There's also highly enjoyable friction on the stomachs and nipples of both partners, and the rubbing of the clitoris against the bed for her (or the penis of the penetrated partner during gay sex).

What's wrong with it? See above – it can result in less sensation for the guy. The woman will find it hard to reach her clitoris or, if the sex is between homosexual men, the recipient won't easily be able to stimulate his penis manually.

Variations on the theme Do it in front of a mirror so you can see each other's face and talk to each other while you make love.

The jigsaw

How to do it She lies on her side and draws her knees up to her chest. He nuzzles into her back and takes her from behind.

What's right with it? She can masturbate herself, or he can play with her clitoris and breasts, while she can clench her buttocks to massage the base of his penis. It's also very intimate and nurturing – he can hold her and whisper in her ear. Two men in this position will both have access to the penis of the penetrated partner and be able to caress his balls.

What's wrong with it? It can be hard for him to build up a good deep thrust, and he might crush his partner's thighs. Movement can be restricted for both of you and you might lose a little of the delicious friction that helps you both reach orgasm. Get round this by wearing a ribbed condom that will enhance sensation.

Variations on the theme If she pulls her legs in towards her chest, she will shorten the rectal passage, making penetration shallower. Or why not try doing the Jigsaw in front of a mirror for even greater intimacy?

6

erotic
massage

Intimate treats

Make your sensual massage a truly relaxing experience by paying special attention to your surroundings. You'll need plenty of time and space – the massage won't work in a cluttered room or if you're constantly interrupted by the telephone. Throw plain white sheets or pretty saris over bookshelves or walls to create a calm, neutral atmosphere, and play soft, ambient, unsyncopated music: it's a fact that slow music actually slows down our breathing and heart rates.

The person being massaged should lie on a firm surface covered by soft sheets or towels – the floor or a futon is fine. It works best if he or she is nude, as stray bra straps and knicker elastic aren't conducive to the flowing, continuous strokes that are the secret of a successful massage. The masseur/se can get naked as well; this helps intimacy and makes it possible to incorporate the whole body, not just the hands, into the massage. Have plenty of fluffy white towels to hand to recreate the pampering atmosphere of the professional spa, to wipe off excess massage oil or to cover the person being massaged: it's essential to keep warm throughout the massage. You might need to turn up the heating, too.

Smell is crucial. Light incense or burn essential oils: aromatherapy will go a long way to creating the atmosphere you want. Essential oils can be uplifting, relaxing or aphrodisiac (see opposite). For the massage itself, you can use baby oil or cosmetic body oil, but your best bet is a custom-made massage oil – preferably neutral, such as peachnut, so that you can add the essential oil of your choice. Essential oils are so powerful that most of them can't be applied neat to the skin.

Massage is a great way to build up physical intimacy and release tension.

The sexiest essential oils

Essential oils are quite volatile and can go off if they're exposed to direct sunlight or heat. Store them in a cool dark place, in dark glass or amber bottles (most of them come in these types of containers). All of the following oils have aphrodisiac effects as well as their unique mood-enhancing properties. A word of warning: you should avoid them altogether if you are — or think you might be — pregnant.

● Basil will wake you up and clear your head. It's great if you want to start the day with a nice massage, especially if you're hoping to get in the mood for sex afterwards. This oil is particularly recommended if you've been feeling sluggish lately.

● Bergamot is used to treat skin problems like acne and eczema, so choose this oil if your skin needs soothing — the end result will be soft, pampered skin and a feeling of wellbeing.

● Clary sage is a sedative and good for PMS. This is a great one to use on a woman who's stressed, especially round day 20 of her menstrual cycle.

● Eucalyptus can relieve cystitis, so if you know you're prone to bladder or kidney infections, treat yourself to this oil. It's a strong smelling and uplifting one, which makes it good to use with vigorous massage techniques.

● Lavender is one of the most powerful and versatile oils, and can also be used neat on the skin to treat spots or delicate skin. Highly aphrodisiac and very relaxing, especially for men, it's been shown to raise testosterone levels. This oil is ideal for stressed and busy couples.

● Rose is the ultimate oil for a night-time or special occasion massage. Neat rose oil is very expensive so you might want to treat yourself to a blend. The smell is evocative of romance; it's a great aphrodisiac as well as being soothing and relaxing.

● Neroli comes from orange blossom and is used to help treat insomnia, which makes it perfect for relaxing or winding down after a stressful week. It results in a real boost to circulation, too: not only will this give you a healthy glow, but it will also help blood flow to the genitals.

● Sandalwood is loved by men because of its musky, masculine smell. Aromatherapists use it to treat low libido and impotence because of its strong relaxing properties.

● Ylang ylang is a powerful anti-depressant, and is recommended if you want to enjoy an intimate conversation during your massage.

Sensual Strokes

An erotic massage has a different objective to traditional massage: it is about intimacy and arousal. Think of each swoop of your hand as a kiss, relaxing and placating your lover. It can be a fabulous part of foreplay, or enjoyed for its own sake. Agree beforehand whether or not you want this to lead to intercourse – if you get carried away, you can always change your mind…

The techniques you'll be using are the three basic strokes from the most widely used massage technique in the Western world: Swiss massage. As your knowledge of these strokes grows, so will your confidence and expertise. Before you begin, it's crucial that your hands are clean, warm and free of jewellery. You should also warm the oil between your hands before you touch your partner, and keep replenishing it to ensure that your hands are always gliding smoothly over your lover's body. As you'll soon find out, the hairier your partner, the more massage oil you're going to need!

Effleurage

This technique involves long, gliding strokes and is used at the beginning of a session to warm up your partner's muscles, or at the end to calm them down again. Use the whole of your hands flat on your partner's body, with equal pressure coming down through the palms and the fingers. Contact should never be broken between your hands and your lover's body. Keep on moving: imagine how annoying it would be if you couldn't listen to your favourite song without it stopping and starting without warning. It's the same during massage – keep at least one hand on your partner's body at all times. Used lightly, effleurage can tickle and tease; medium strokes will relax and promote sleep; more vigorous ones will stimulate and invigorate. Constantly ask your partner what feels good.

Your hands have 72,000 nerve endings. If you concentrate on how good your partner feels under your fingertips, you'll be more sensitive and you'll both notice the difference. As you get used to giving a massage, you'll learn to feel your way around your lover's body, to look for signs of tension and to listen for little clicks in bone and muscle that show you where he or she is stressed.

Petrissage

This is a more invigorating technique and involves kneading, squeezing and rolling fleshy areas of the body such as the stomach, thighs and buttocks. Take a portion of soft tissue between the thumb and fingers of one or both hands, and then think of kneading dough: roll and squeeze the flesh between your hands. You can use your body weight to lean into the strokes. Ask your partner to let you know whether the pressure you're using is too much or too little.

Performed regularly and firmly, petrissage can break down fatty tissues and help problems like cellulite. It's also great for stiff or sprained muscles as it gets the blood flowing here again. Don't use this technique on the face because it's too intense for the delicate skin here; it should also be avoided on the abdomen of pregnant women.

Friction

Use the pads of your thumbs to make tiny circles on your partner's skin. You'll often need to use your body weight here to provide the pressure required for this precise stroke. It's best for those tight muscle spots you noticed during the effleurage. This stroke may not sound too sexy, but the more relaxed your partner's muscles are, the more likely he or she is to be primed for orgasm – and supple enough to try the most adventurous sex positions! You can also vary the pressure of the stroke: after a vigorous rub, your fingertip circles can be profoundly arousing.

Additional strokes

If you've mastered the three basic techniques of effleurage, petrissage and friction, you might also like to try the following strokes, which will help you vary the massage routine:

Cupping Make your hands into little cups and drum them up and down along your partner's back. If you're doing it right you should produce a hollow 'clop clop' sound, not a slapping sound.

Pounding Use the fleshy underside of your fist to stimulate areas such as the buttocks and thighs.

Pinching Use lots of light pinching movements on your partner's skin. This teases as well as gets the blood flowing to the surface of the skin – a good method to use if the massage is a prelude to sex.

Stillness Sometimes it can be incredibly intimate to just stop what you're doing and place your hands flat on your lover's body and let the warmth pass between you.

Thai massage

This soapy sex secret from Southeast Asia is fast catching on in the West: it's a full-body massage with a difference. It's usually given to a man by a woman, but with care it can be performed on a woman by a man, and is great for a treat on a hot summer night or on holiday.

Thai massage involves lots of soap and water, so move out of the bedroom and into the bathroom. She lathers herself up with soapsuds while he lies on his front on a couple of towels on the floor. Once she's feeling foamy and frisky, she lies face down on his back and slips, slides and writhes up and down his body. He then turns over and she repeats the movements on his front. If he wants to return the favour, he should prop up his weight on his forearms, as he does when he's in the missionary position. Obviously if one or both of you is very heavy, you should be careful when giving a Thai massage!

from top to toe

Each part of the body responds differently to different types of touch. Here you'll find an all-over massage routine that can last for up to 90 minutes. You don't have to follow this particular order or complete the whole programme – and by all means feel free to pay extra attention to your partner's favourite erogenous zones. You can also incorporate any of these techniques into your regular foreplay routine.

Face and scalp

Use your middle and index fingers to massage the temples in gentle circular motions. Sweep your thumb and forefingers across your partner's eyebrows and closed eyelids. Concentrate on the area around the mouth as the nerve endings surrounding the lips are very near the surface, providing a short cut to sexual arousal. The hair follicles on the scalp make it one of the most responsive areas on the body. Use all of your fingers to make small, circular motions, about 2 cm wide. This technique, borrowed from the tradition of Shiatsu massage, can have incredibly relaxing effects and has been known to send some people to sleep.

Neck and shoulders

Sit astride your partner's buttocks before you start on the neck and shoulders, the area where many of us carry most of our stress and tension. The right touch here can melt the frostiest ice queen in

seconds, as the skin in this area is thin and highly responsive. Begin with your palms resting on the point where the neck meets the shoulders and drag slowly outwards, kneading the skin as you go. Everyone's different, so ask your partner if he or she wants more or less pressure. Using both hands, work your way from the neck outwards with short, strong squeezing movements. Also try tracing your knuckles along the top 5 cm of the spine.

Back

Take advantage of the fact that we can't reach our own backs, so we're all crying out for attention here. Place both hands palms down on the shoulders and move them firmly in opposing circles. Work out and away from the spine, progressing down the back and over the buttocks, then work back up to the shoulders and repeat twice. Other great strokes for the back include alternate kneading (gentle squeezing of your partner's flesh with each hand in turn). Also try thumbing (short, rapid, alternate strokes with your thumbs). The slower you take this the better, especially for women: less is more on delicate female skin, and the lighter and gentler your touch, the more turned-on she'll be. Guys, if you're getting turned-on too, tease her by running your erection up and down her spine.

Bottom

Because we can't reach them and we spend so much time sitting on them, our bottoms are much-neglected erogenous zones. Your partner will be particularly appreciative of a bottom massage if he or she has an office or deskbound job. Begin at the top of the buttocks, with your fingertips touching and your elbows pointing outwards, and move down firmly, kneading deeply with the palms. For real deep relief, make fists and swirl them on your partner's bottom. Give the sacrum a stroke. This small dent just above the crease of the bum is extremely responsive when massaged in a circular motion with your thumb. Don't be afraid to use both your thumbs to smooth along the crack in between the buttocks – the knock-on relaxing effect will be felt throughout the back and upper body.

Feet

Reflexology – the art of foot massage – also holds the key to unlocking your sexual energy. To limber your partner's feet up and make them more responsive to your touch, hold the top of one foot with your right hand and rotate it several times, first one way and then the other; repeat on the other foot. Our sex drive is directly linked to a pressure point on the inside of the foot about half a centimetre below the anklebone, so cup your partner's heel in one hand and with your other hand place the tip of your middle finger on the pressure point. This is your partner's treat, so you might have to shift the angle of your body to approach him or her from this angle. For the ovaries and testicles, the point is exactly the same on the outside of the foot. Repeat the process once on each side of each foot.

Legs

This part of the body can tolerate quite strong strokes: start just above the ankle and, using your whole palm, smooth the skin all the way up, stopping 12–15 cm away from the bottom. If you want to pay attention to your partner's inner thighs, be warned – this erogenous zone is so sensitive it could lead to intercourse sooner than you'd both planned. Try

using your thumbs to push gently along the back of the legs (where the seams would lie if your lover was wearing old-fashioned stockings); this releases tension and caresses the most sensitive part of the leg at the same time.

Breasts and chests

Now roll over and pay attention to the chest and breast area – men's nipples can be as sensitive as women's, so don't neglect his torso. Tease your partner with delicate strokes using your fingers, thumbs and tongue. Swirl around the breast area, avoiding the nipple for several minutes until she's begging for you to touch it. Finish the chest massage by gently rolling the nipples between your thumb and forefinger, or simply take each one in your mouth for a minute or two.

Stomach

Just place your warm palms (rub your hands together first for the best effect) on your lover's lower abdomen and move very slightly backwards and forwards to send shivers through his or her nether regions. Or show off with the following technique, a favourite of the ancient Chinese (these incredibly forward-thinking people prescribed sexual massage as a treatment for illness). Identifying your 'Rushing Door' sexual acupressure point makes for longer, lustier sex. It lies exactly half-way along the crease at the top of your thigh (the line where your thigh meets your torso) – just hold your first two fingers there for a minute or two. The more you repeat this, the more sexual energy you'll have.

intimate massage

The grand finale to your routine is a hands-on, erotic massage. Caressing your lover's genitals with the same intimate touch you've used on the rest of his or her body can be an incredibly moving and bonding experience. This isn't mutual masturbation – the techniques are different and you're not trying to bring your partner to orgasm. Although if that does occur, it's a nice surprise!

For him

Adjust your position so he can see you as you go to work. He'll love to know you're enjoying playing with his penis as much as he's enjoying the sensation you're giving him. Look rapturous, as though you couldn't think of a more exciting way to keep your hands busy.

● He's quite hairy here so use plenty of lubricant – and make sure you warm it well in your hands first, as cold liquid can make even the proudest of penises shy.

● Don't just go straight for his penis – use your warm wet fingers to explore his whole genital area, firmly stroking the skin around his anus and perineum. Cup his balls in your hands and just hold them there, breathing in time with his breath.

● Remember your golden rule – continuous stimulation and keep your hands on him at all times. Begin by rubbing his penis gently between your hands.

● The warmth of your hands and the lube should make it feel like a long, never-ending, moving vagina. You've got to be firm and swift, and it's important to make sure the tip of his penis is never uncovered for more than a split second at a time.

● Apply the lubricant to your hands and his. Place your hands around his erection, palms facing each other, fingers pointing upwards. He then places his hands over yours and guides them up and down his penis.

● If it looks like he's going to come before you've had a chance to show him all the tricks you've got up your sleeve, squeeze the tip of his penis. Use your thumb and forefinger to put gentle pressure on the top and bottom of his penis, just underneath the head. (Don't squeeze the head itself, however: it's so sensitive, you'll either hurt him or defeat the object of the exercise by bringing him to orgasm there and then!)

● Your *pièce de résistance* is the two-stroke masterpiece. For the first stroke, grasp the top of his penis with your right hand and place the left underneath his balls, with your fingers positioned towards the anus. As you slide your right hand down the penis shaft, enclosing it as much as possible, bring your left hand up from his testicles, so both your hands collide at the base of his penis. For the second stroke, slide your right hand back up his penis from the base while simultaneously bringing your left hand under his balls again – keep going and save this one for last, as it's the big showdown.

For her

This should be done at the end of your massage session – she'll be totally relaxed, and it gives her something to look forward to.

● Sit between her legs, so you've got eye contact and you can talk each other through what you're doing. She can wrap her legs round your head or spread them. She might enjoy sitting up a bit, too.

● An all-too-often neglected rung of any woman's stairway to heaven, the skin on the inner thigh is packed with nerve endings and incredibly sensitive to your touch. Again, tease her by making your touch so light it could almost be an accident you're feeling her at all.

● Trace her outer labia, subtly feeling to see if she's getting wet before you progress. Some 98% of women say they are as sensitive to having the inner lips stroked as they are to having their clitorises stimulated, so lightly touch these as well. Don't be afraid to play with her labia – lightly pull it and then let it go. Do this regularly. Now more than ever it's important for you to keep up that steady rhythm.

● Dribble warm water or massage oil over her genitals, teasing her by letting the liquid run along her clitoris and trickle down her labia. Don't use oil or any other product that isn't designed for intimate use.

● Play with her pubic hair, tugging it gently. This is a subtle tease that gets the blood flowing to the genital area.

● When you touch her clitoris, run your finger so lightly she can barely feel it, all around the skin around the clitoris. Make little circles in both directions. Watch and see her response – often in this case less is more, because if she's relaxed she might find herself coming. Resist the temptation to increase the pace and intensity as you would during masturbation: here the emphasis is on technique.

Your essential massage kit
Nothing beats hand-on-skin contact in an erotic massage, but when you get tired, use these props and toys to help you.

● A vibrator. This isn't just for delivering orgasms! Hold a vibrator, on a low speed, against aching muscles for a fabulous no-effort massage.

● A pearl necklace. Fake is acceptable! Roll the string of pearls along the backs of legs, between the buttocks and around the penis. The pressure of each individual bead will massage and stimulate.

● Heat-activated massage oil. When you don't want to create warmth and friction with your fingers, apply this to your lover's skin and gently blow on it. It heats up, enhancing even the lightest of touches.

7

the Secrets of tantra

what is tantric Sex?

The *Tantras* are ancient Hindu and Buddhist scriptures that take the form of a dialogue between the god Shiva and his wife Shakti, providing teachings on – among other subjects – meditation, spiritual knowledge and sexual rituals. The word 'tantra' is Sanskrit, and translates as 'the way' – in this case, a very enjoyable way to worship! Tantric sex is a totally different approach to lovemaking. If Western sex is a thrilling rush towards one particular goal – orgasm – Tantric sex is like an interesting journey that's enjoyable for its own sake. The emphasis is on delaying orgasm and merging with your lover… body, mind and spirit.

The idea of male and female energies becoming one is at the heart of Tantric philosophy. Partners are encouraged to explore the opposite aspects of their nature during sex, so the woman can take a dynamic role while her partner relinquishes the initiative and relaxes into his softer, more feminine side. By allowing these male and female energies to merge, you achieve a sacred union and create a powerful, loving and ecstatic force, connecting you to a higher consciousness.

Tantric practitioners believe that every time a man ejaculates, he loses vital energy, so the aim of Tantric sex is to delay the male orgasm for as long as possible (to conserve that energy) or avoid it altogether (to transform that energy into an inner spiritual bliss). Advanced disciples of Tantra spend years meditating and studying yoga to reach this state, and it's not something that can be recreated or summarised here. Instead, over the next few pages is an introduction to the principles of Tantra, and exercises that will bring you sex that's more intimate, thoughtful and long lasting than you've ever known.

The chakras

As with any journey, you'll need a map, and in this case the map is of your body. According to Tantric philosophy, there are seven energy centres in the body known as chakras. Each chakra is located in a particular part of the body, is associated with a particular colour and corresponds with a certain spiritual, physical and emotional state, as follows:

1 The base chakra, in the pelvis, is the centre of sexual desire and childbirth. Its colour is red.

2 The sacral chakra, just below the navel, is the centre of balance, movement and stability. Its colour is orange.

3 The solar plexus chakra, at the bottom of the rib case, is the centre of self-confidence and charisma. Its colour is yellow.

4 The heart chakra, between the nipples, is the centre of love, sharing, trust, compassion and joy. Its colour is green.

5 The throat chakra, on the throat, is the centre of self-knowledge and expression. Its colour is blue.

6 The brow chakra, between the eyes, is the centre of imagination and perception. Its colour is purple.

7 The crown chakra, located just above the crown of the head, is the centre of spiritual connection and ecstasy. Its colour is violet.

The chakras can be either open or closed. To reach a supreme state of consciousness, all seven energy centres must be fully open – and Tantric followers believe it is possible to achieve this through sexual union. For an exercise to help open your chakras, see page 117.

Solo Spirituality
sacred rituals for one

It's important to prepare for Tantric sex from the inside, through exercises and meditation. The good news is that this preparation for love-making doesn't involve showering, shaving or deciding what to wear. The holistic approach means the only work you have to do beforehand is to get to know yourself better. And the best way to achieve the tranquillity you need to do just this is through meditation.

This meditation programme is about becoming comfortable with your own sexuality before you lay one finger on your lover. Breathing properly is the key to successful Tantra. We all know that breathing keeps us alive, but learning to control our breathing taps into our sexual selves and helps us to control the timing and power of our orgasms. The more fully and deeply we breathe, the more alive we are. It works on another

Think of meditation as spiritual foreplay you can do on your own.

level as well: by concentrating on our breathing and nothing else, we forget the trivial but totally human everyday worries about the way we look, feel, smell or taste. The senses become totally unselfconscious and open up to new sexual experiences.

Do whatever it is you need to be comfortable in your own skin. Lie in the sunlight if that makes you feel good, or surround yourself with tiny candles. Lie on a silk or cotton throw that feels comfortable and natural yet sensual underneath you. Certain essential oils will also help to concentrate and subtly prime your body for sex. Try mixing cedarwood, frankincense and rose essential oils.

● Dedicate a small area of your home as a sacred space. This should be somewhere warm and comfortable – but preferably not your bed as you equate this with a very different kind of relaxation.

● Lie down and close your eyes. Think about each body part and the wonderful effect oxygen is having on it as you breathe in and out.

● Keep breathing, but now inhale and exhale as deeply and as slowly as you can.

● Imagine you hear the breath of another person inches away from you, and that you and they are breathing in total synchronicity.

● Still breathing deeply, visualise that other person blowing warm or cool air all over your body.

● Think about the air and how it feels on your hair and skin.

Take time out to do this every day. If you can't spend a little time in your designated meditation area, block out the outside world and breathe deeply wherever you can.

Focus your mind on the positive by making a list of all the things in your life that bring you pleasure. Begin with the non-sexual: things you love about your job, your home, films, books, friends who light up your life. Now do the same for specific sexual pleasures: the taste of your lover's skin, the way he or she feels during intercourse, how great it feels when you touch yourself, the colour of your lover's hair. Whenever your attention wanders to the niggles of everyday life, return to the awareness of your breathing and nothing else.

Start with 15 minutes of meditation each day and work up to half an hour. Set your radio alarm clock to a classical music station to bring you back into the present at the end of each session. Take time out to relax back into your surroundings before you get up and resume normal life.

the power of two

meditations and exercises for lovers

When you practise Tantric sex, you're entering a holistic relationship, which means you're committing yourself with mind, body and spirit. This involves knowing, and accepting, everything about your partner. Even if you're having passionate sex every night, or you've been living together for ten years, there will still be aspects of your lover you have yet to discover. This can be a daunting experience, which is why the following exercises are designed to help you understand each other spiritually as well as physically.

The early stages of this Tantric programme focus on the mind and spirit aspects of Tantra rather than the body. Before your bodies can merge into one, you must first achieve an awareness of your partner's emotional and spiritual existence. For this reason you must avoid nudity or provocative clothing. Both of you should dress in loose clothing, in a natural fibre such as cotton, preferably white. If you prefer to do these exercises in your underwear, that too should be plain and white.

Caressing meditation

This simple meditation between two lovers is a good exercise to begin with if you're new to Tantra, as it's incredibly calm and gentle. Take it in turns to be passive and active, to give and receive this massage. The passive partner lies back on the bed with his or her eyes closed, while the active partner gently caresses him or her from head to toe. Use the three middle fingers and concentrate on every inch of the body apart from the genitals. Keep stroking and

caressing for twenty minutes. While you're caressing your partner, visualise him or her as a god or prince, goddess or princess, and think of your caresses as a gift of worship.

Chakra meditation

Sit facing away from each other in your meditation space. Your legs should be crossed and your backs touching, your spines relaxed but still erect, your shoulders back and your hands in your laps, palms upwards. Breathe deeply in each other's presence for five minutes.

Coordinate your breathing so that you're both inhaling and exhaling as one, and then begin to focus on each chakra in turn. Start with the base chakra, which is located in your pelvis. Focus on that part of your body and think about the emotions and energies associated with this energy centre – sexual pleasure, reproduction and childbirth. Visualise the rich reds and ochres of the chakra. Let the colour flood your mind and fill your inner eye. Repeat the same process for each chakra, spending about three minutes on each one. When your meditation is over, allow yourselves five minutes to wind down, still breathing in time with each other.

Meditation of the five senses

This is a real gift of a meditation as one partner lies back and enjoys the experience while the other treats him or her to a series of sensual experiences. This meditation helps to train and focus all five senses, and participants often report a greater all-round sensory appreciation of lovemaking afterwards. It can be really fun for the 'active' partner, whose job it is to find the suitable sexy surprises needed for this meditation.

The passive partner is blindfolded, and lies back, propped up on pillows awaiting the experiences their lover has prepared. With their sight dulled, they will become more sensually responsive to the other four senses of touch, taste, smell and sound, which the active partner should stimulate as follows:

Smell Shake a few drops of an essential oil onto a silk handkerchief and place it under your partner's nose. Natural smells, from flowers or fresh herbs, can also be used.

Sound Whisper sweet nothings into your partner's ear or treat them to the sound of your breathing. Say whatever comes naturally. Calmly tell them how beautiful they look, and how close to them you feel at this point in time.

Taste Put fresh, natural foods to your partner's lips. Vary the tastes and textures, using fresh fruit (strawberries and banana are great favourites here) and savoury foods with different textures, such as roasted peppers and olives.

Touch Keep your partner on high alert by tracing your hand in slow, sensual movements all over them, jumping from one part of the body to another so you'll keep them guessing as to where the next caress will be coming from.

Sight Take off your own clothes, whip off the blindfold and stand still, letting your lover see and appreciate your naked body.

Mother–child meditation

This allows men to be vulnerable, which society often discourages. It's also a great opportunity for a woman to be totally feminine in a way that isn't necessarily sexual. She holds him in her arms while he curls up in her lap and sucks her breasts. He suckles as a baby would with his mother, not as he would to arouse his lover during foreplay or sexual intercourse.

tantric loving
step by step

You won't be ready for intercourse until you've spent a while – ideally three days – meditating and learning to breathe in harmony together. The evening before your Tantric lovemaking, perform one last meditation together. Sit side by side, stroking each other everywhere on your bodies, lingering near the genitals but not touching them. The purpose of your touch is definitely to arouse, but on no condition may you caress your lover intimately. Even if you're moaning, shaking and sweating with frustration, do not allow yourselves sexual release. Instead, focus on controlling your breathing, making the breaths deep, slow and even. That evening, sleep in each other's arms but don't caress one another or kiss.

The object of this exercise is to control your bodies by letting sexual feeling build and then subside.

Arousing rituals

Before you start to make love, take a bath or shower together and massage sensual aromatherapy oils into each other's skin. Practitioners of Tantra thousands of years ago would 'anoint' their partners before making love, to remind themselves that sexual intercourse was part of a religious ritual. As you anoint your lover, again imagine that they are the embodiment of a god or goddess, but always retain an awareness that this person is your lover. Tantric sex is the absolute opposite of dressing up and fantasising to reach orgasm – instead, turn your thoughts to everything you love and desire about the person you're with.

Continue by synchronising your breathing. Mastering this is the single most important part of Tantric sex. Lie in the spoons position so that your ribcages are touching one another and you can feel every movement, every inhalation and exhalation. After twenty minutes or so of lying like this, turn so that you're facing your lover. Either lie on your sides, with your foreheads almost touching, or sit cross-legged opposite one another. Look long over your lover's face, registering the beauty of each contour. Notice every single eyelash

and eyebrow hair, and the many different colours in the irises of their eyes. When you have gazed at your partner's face for five minutes, make eye contact and don't break it until intercourse is over.

Kiss, but not so passionately that you're clawing at each other's body and gasping for air. The emphasis should be on taking in your lover's breath. Take it in turns to hold the other person's lower lip between your own, and run your tongue slowly across his or her teeth. Take time to hold still, lips together, and let yourselves be. Visualise that each breath is taken in through alternate nostrils.

Make a slow, sensual connection between your lips.

Sit opposite each other and stroke each other's chest and shoulders, then each other's back, drawing your bodies closer as you do so. As you touch your partner, imagine what it must be like to feel the strokes you're administering. Touch his or her thigh, and imagine that your own thigh is receiving a lover's caress. This technique harnesses the power of your imagination and trains you to focus instinctively on your partner's pleasure as well as your own.

Progress to gently stroking one another's genitals, imagining how it would feel if you had a penis or a vagina – whichever you don't have. If you feel orgasm approaching, delay it by repeating the word *lingam* if your partner is male (*lingam* means 'wand of light' in Sanskrit, and represents the penis), or *yoni* ('sacred place' or vagina) if your partner is female. Keep up the genital touching for three minutes and then rest for five, breathing in synch.

You're now ready for penetration. The man should lie on his back, while the woman lowers herself on to his erection. Slowly, slowly, with both of you concentrating on your breathing throughout, she should lean her upper body forward and extend her legs so that she is lying face down on top of him with his penis snug inside her vagina. Stay utterly still – concentrate not on the physical sensations in your genitals but on breathing together. Remain like this until he loses his erection. When this happens, the woman should gently rock her pelvis or clench her PC muscle to stimulate him. As his penis becomes fully erect, she should place her head on his chest and once again, both of you should focus on your breathing. The woman can rock gently to stimulate her clitoris and vagina. By keeping her movements small and slow, she can increase her own arousal without overstimulating him. It's vital that the man's climax is delayed until the woman is orgasmic. It's also important that neither of you is tempted to resume the thrusting nor fast, shallow breathing that accompanies your regular lovemaking. If this happens (and it's only natural that it will, the first few times you make love in the Tantric way) return to stillness.

Hints for men: how to delay ejaculation

As you feel your orgasm approaching during intercourse, your instinct is probably to thrust faster and deeper. But with practice, you can learn to make love in the slow, shallow movements needed to delay your climax and facilitate hers.

● When you have sexual feelings, visualise them moving up through each chakra and spreading throughout your whole body rather than allowing them to be concentrated in the pelvis. Think about the location, the colour and the nature of each chakra, breathing deeply into each one as you do.

● Try to remain in the moment and concentrate on her and her pleasure, and on adoring her. Use this thought to stay in the plateau stage of sexual arousal and stave off orgasm.

● Instead of letting the sphincter in your penis release the semen, contract the sphincter in your anus. This will in turn lead you to clench your PC muscle, inhibiting ejaculation.

● You can also pull down gently on your balls to control ejaculation: they naturally rise up in your body when you climax but won't be able to if you're holding onto them.

● If you really think you're going to come, arch your spine, lift your head upwards and breathe in deeply, at the same time applying pressure with the index and middle finger of your left hand on your perineum, the area between your balls and anus. This will inhibit the flow of semen from the prostate gland.

● According to Tantric philosophy, the woman's natural juice is the most powerful energy source. Concentrate on absorbing her lubrication, and think of the extra energy you're gaining.

● Press your tongue on the roof of your mouth while steadying your thoughts and breath, or roll up your tongue and use it like a straw to breathe in cooling air.

● If any of these techniques are too successful and you lose your erection, try 'soft entry sex': use your hands to place your soft penis inside your lover's vagina. She can then squeeze while you thrust until your penis is erect again.

Positions for prolonging the pleasure

Certain poses lend themselves more readily to Tantric lovemaking than others; the following encourage intimacy and inhibit movement, which is necessary if he's to delay his orgasm. They're especially designed to help you feel each other's breathing rhythms and synchronise your breathing. But part of the fun of exploring Tantra is creating your own love rituals and making the experience personal. Why not create your own secret names for your favourite positions?

Yab-yum

This position is easy to move into from the back-stroking exercise on page 120. He kneels or sits with his legs crossed, while she wraps her arms around his neck and her legs around his waist, and gently takes his erection inside her.

Tantric practitioners believe that if a man's spine is erect during intercourse, he's able to moderate his passion. It's true that he's not likely to climax too soon, as this is a fantastic position for letting him focus not on his own pleasure but on that of his partner. Yab-yum facilitates eye contact and harmonised breathing, which is all the communication you need. Don't speak to one another.

For as long as you can manage, the woman should keep up just enough pelvic movement to keep his penis erect inside her. If he's becoming overstimulated, she can raise her legs over his shoulders. This offers her the deeper penetration she needs, while the top of her vagina is stretched and lengthened by this position, denying him the stimulation at the tip of the penis that might trip him over into premature climax.

When you've finished intercourse and both been satisfied, remain in the yab-yum position, breathing harmoniously, until his penis is totally limp. Next, bow down to each other: kneel opposite one another, stretch your arms out in front of you, and place your head on the floor or bed. This serves as a 'thank you' to your lover, and reminds the two of you that what you've just done was a meditation. As you bow down, think about the fact that although your bodies have become two again, for a while you were united in intercourse. Ending your lovemaking with a deep bow will help you remember it as a spiritual as well as a sexual experience.

The inverted embrace

This woman-on-top position begins with the man lying on his back. She sits astride him, lowering herself onto his erection if he has one or taking the first inch or so of his flaccid penis into her vagina if he doesn't, and using her vaginal muscles to stimulate him until he is erect. Once he's inside her, she slides her legs backwards and extends her upper body forwards and downwards until she's lying face down on him, hands resting on his chest, her head resting wherever it falls naturally. She then lies still except for making almost imperceptible rocking movements with her pelvis that subtly stimulate her clitoris. If he becomes overexcited, roll onto your sides and lie in this position for a while – this will greatly decrease the stimulation as well as the depth of penetration. As she senses her own orgasm approaching, he tightens his buttocks and swivels his hips in a tiny figure-of-eight movement. This results in a pleasant 'corkscrew' move-ment for her and an enhanced orgasm for him. Making love in this position with her legs pulled up makes penetration deeper and allows easier access to her G-spot. She can also bear down upon him and gently, subtly, rub her clitoris against his pubic bone, increasing her chances of orgasm.

8

deliciously
kinky

fantasies

We all use fantasy in aspects of our everyday lives, even if it's only a daydream about what we'd do if we won the lottery. And we all indulge in sexual fantasies on some level, whether that's imagining how the handsome new guy in accounts would look naked, or wondering what it would be like to go into that sex shop we pass on the way to work every day, rather than just staring at it curiously.

We're more aware of fantasising when we masturbate than at other times – replaying images in our heads of people and situations, real and imagined. Most of us use our imaginations to help us reach orgasm when we're alone, and many of us use fantasy to turn ourselves on when we're with our partners. We fantasise about things we just wouldn't dream of doing in real life – group or gay sex, sex with our partner's friends and colleagues, sex with our own friends and colleagues. That's why they're called fantasies… and they're totally normal.

Most of us never share our sexual fantasies, worrying what our friends or partners might think. But you can bet that whatever's going on in your head, there's something equally smutty going on in theirs! We also worry that confessing our fantasies means our lovers will think we prefer what's happening in our heads to what's happening between the sheets. But the truth is that if you talk about your deepest desires and share them in the right way, it can make for absolutely mind-blowing sex. Some popular fantasies are so simple they can be acted out with the minimum of fuss – sex in the open air, for example, or anal sex. All it takes to get them out in the open is a little frank conversation.

Men's top ten fantasies

1 Sex with an anonymous woman

2 Sex with two women at once, one of whom is his partner

3 Watching another couple have sex

4 Sleeping with a prostitute

5 Anal sex with a woman

6 An erotic encounter with another man

7 Having sex while people watch/group sex

8 Being dominated

9 Watching another man have intercourse with his lover

10 Being tied up or restrained during sex

Sharing fantasies can enrich your lovemaking by allowing you to experiment with different behaviours.

Women's top ten fantasies

1. Sex with partner
2. Sex with a stranger
3. Sex with a celebrity/friend/acquaintance/colleague
4. Sex with another woman
5. Sex before an audience
6. Watching another couple make love
7. Being tied up or restrained during sex
8. Sex as a 'punishment'
9. Sex with a faceless, anonymous man
10. Group sex

Sit down and discuss your fantasies before you go to work on enacting them. If this is new territory for you, take a look at the lists opposite and above of men and women's favourite fantasies. Which ideas turn you on? If you like the idea of power and submission, think about scenarios in which you could play this out – sexual positions which would involve you surrendering all control, for example, or words you could say to exercise power over your partner. Explore the different roles you could play – master and servant, politician and intern – that would fulfil this fantasy.

Before you start, though, bear in mind that your fantasies might lose their value if they're acted out. Some are better left as reveries. There are also some fantasies that just shouldn't be dumped on a lover – if you can't stop thinking about your husband's brother, say, will it really enhance your relationship if you tell your husband? While honesty is important, you don't need to know everything about each other. Keep something back for yourself. Only share a fantasy if you're absolutely sure it will enrich your relationship.

Dressing up and role-play

Acting out a scenario and assuming 'characters' during sex doesn't mean you don't want to make love to each other any more – just that you're both going to adopt a different persona for a short while. Once you've decided on a storyline that excites both of you, set aside an evening to indulge your fantasy. Plan ahead, thinking about every little detail of the clothes you'll wear and the props you'll use. The more details you get right, the more you can lose yourselves in the thrill of the fantasy. Fuel your imaginations by dressing up to act out your fantasies. Any kind of change is a libido-booster, but there's no bigger turn-on than seeing your partner dressed up purely (or impurely) for your mutual pleasure.

If you've never done any kind of role-play before, start by pretending to be strangers in a bar and picking each other up. This will gradually work you into the idea of role-play without needing any fancy costumes – or indeed anything more than the price of a drink and a cab fare home. You'll also both be 'you' – just as strangers, as you were when you first met.

Whatever your fantasy, one of the following ideas for role-play will suit you. Some of them require little more than everyday clothes and household objects, others are a little more specialised.

Baby games Cuddle up to each other and revert to childlike speech. Dress each other in nappies and make love on a rubber sheet. Bathe each other like babies and feed each other baby food. Some people take this further and wee all over each other – try this in the shower before you embark on a massive clean-up operation. Alternatively, play mother-and-child games where the woman 'breast-feeds' her lover.

French dominatrix So you've invested in some leather lingerie to play the dominatrix. Get into your role. What's the dominatrix's name? How does she speak? Maybe she's foreign – that would really be exotic and erotic. Even if you haven't spoken French since you were a schoolgirl, learn some sexy phrases to arouse him. For more ideas on how to play the dominatrix, turn to pages 133–38.

Boss and employee Sex in the office is a hugely popular fantasy – money and power are strong aphrodisiacs after all. Turn your dining-room table into an executive office by placing a laptop computer on the top and scattering the surface with official-looking documents (even if it's just your own phone bill). Wear normal office clothes with outrageous lingerie underneath and undress each other so fast that you rip all the buttons off your shirts.

Personal trainer and client This is a ready-made power relationship, with one of you ordering the other person to 'drop and give me twenty' – only instead of push-ups, you're demanding sexual favours. Set a stopwatch to time your intercourse. Dress in sports gear that leaves little to the imagination. To add an extra twist, why not begin your lovemaking session with a couple of hours at the gym to work up a sweat?

Hooker and client Maybe you'd like to dress up in expensive lingerie and pose as a hooker to excite your lover? If so, develop a character for your after-hours alter ego. What's her speciality? How much does she charge for masturbation, oral or full intercourse? Have him bring along some dollar bills or Monopoly money to add authenticity. Hire a sleazy hotel room for an hour: a change of scenery can only enhance your role-play. If you can't get to a hotel, get out of the bedroom and make love on the stairs, the living-room floor, the kitchen table… anywhere that you don't associate with your day-to-day sex life.

Dracula and the virgin He dresses as Count Dracula in a cape and fake fangs while she wears a long white robe. He nuzzles her neck while she pretends she's not sure if she really, really wants to – although of course she does! Remember, fantasy is supposed to be fun: adopt Transylvanian accents and challenge each other not to get the giggles. Take the fantasy further but keep it safe by buying some fake blood from a joke shop and smearing it all over each other's necks and bodies.

Nurse and patient If you're playing the nurse – complete with the kind of revealing, PVC uniform never provided by the NHS – give your patient a thorough examination to find out what's the matter with him. Surprise him by slipping an ice-cold stethoscope (get a fake one from a children's toyshop) where he's least expecting it (try this on the underside of his balls and drive him wild). Your bedside manner is all-important. Talk him through what you're doing to him using clinical, anatomical words. No matter how aroused you get, try to keep your voice calm and professional at all times.

His 'n' hers Try swapping clothes and cross-dressing. Experience what its like to be on the other side of the gender divide and the sexual floodgates will open. Whoever normally wears the trousers in bed might find that, dressed in their lover's underwear, they feel the need to submit to the other's desires for a change. The different feel of strange clothes against your skin can be a turn-on in itself.

threesomes and moresomes

Most couples think of sex as a private experience between the two of them. Many of these may fantasise about threesomes, group sex parties and 'swinging' (swapping sexual partners), but relatively few act on those fantasies. There are, however, couples who think monogamy is unrealistic and undesirable and don't follow its rules – indeed, it's the fact that our monogamous society frowns on sex with more than one person that provides the biggest turn-on.

Threesomes – a couple inviting a third party to join them in bed – consistently rate high in the fantasy polls, and it's one of the easiest fantasies to fulfil, requiring nothing more than three consenting adults. However, threesomes will only work in practice if both of you are utterly secure in your relationship and totally immune to jealousy (and how many of us can say that?). The *idea* of seeing your lover rolling around in bed with someone else might be incredibly sexy, but the *reality* of it, and the aftermath, can wreck relationships. Indulge the fantasy by having sex in front of a mirror to create the illusion of there being more people in bed with you.

Group sex is nothing new, but it came into its own in the 1960s and 1970s, when the pill and more relaxed social mores led to greater sexual spontaneity. Its popularity waned a little during the 1980s with the advent of AIDS, but it is currently undergoing a renaissance: the swinging scene is back with a vengeance.

What's the appeal of group sex? Well, there's a certain exhibitionist pleasure to be enjoyed from having sex in front of an audience, and of course there's the voyeuristic thrill you get from watching others doing it. From a practical point of view, you can learn lots of new tricks through watching other people make love. There are as many variations on group sex as there are participants, and everyone has their own particular turn-on. Some people like to watch their partners have intercourse with other men and women;

some like to reach out and touch someone else while they're having sex with their partner; others just enjoy the anonymous thrill of not knowing whether it's a man or a woman that's touching them.

That said, group sex is complicated and controversial. Almost all couples who are into swinging only do it within some kind of confines – whether that's a club where group sex is permitted, at a pre-arranged 'wife swapping' party, or with other couples they know and trust enough to swing with. But this means you have to build up some kind of relationship with other people, so anonymity is no longer possible; it also leaves room for jealousy to fester. Many couples create rules for themselves to keep possible problems in check – many insist on no eye contact. Then again, a lot of swingers get off on risk as much as anything else. If this isn't a chance you're willing to take to fulfil your fantasies, try watching group sex films together instead, which will provide lots of excitement without the risks.

The sight, sound and smell of other people making love can be very arousing.

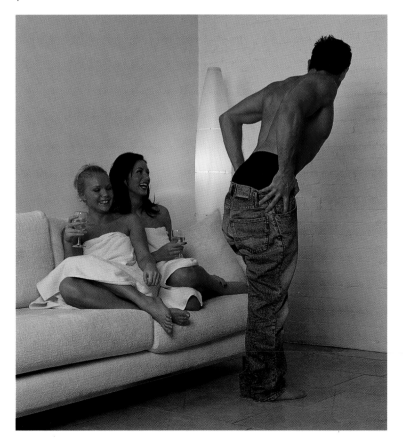

bondage

This is the act of being physically restrained during sex, and its appeal is about fantasy and the illusion of helplessness. Some people love to dominate their lovers during sex: others want nothing more than to submit to their partner's every whim.

Provided bondage takes place between eager, consenting adults, who know what they're doing, there's no reason why it shouldn't become an enjoyable part of their sex lives. Tying-up games can provide a fun, safe, sexy outlet for the feelings of sexual power, rivalry and frustration that we all experience in relationships.

Not sure whether you want to be the one who's tied up or the one who does the tying up? Most of us naturally gravitate towards one role or the other, but if you can't decide, think about which scenario turns you on more: acting as your partner's sex slave for the evening, or having your lover kiss your boots in worship and obedience. If the first turns you on, you're a natural submissive (also known as a sub) and you'll be the one who gets a kick out of being chained to the bedposts. If the second one arouses you, you're a dominant (or dom) and you'll be the one who has the keys to the handcuffs!

Bondage for beginners

Are you sitting uncomfortably? Good. Then we'll begin. A lot of people think that bondage is all about inflicting pain on a partner, and shy away. It's true that some people do enjoy light pain as part of their lovemaking, but if you're not comfortable with it, there's still room for experimentation.

Test the water by doing something subtle, like holding your partner's hands still during sex so he or she can't move. If it goes down well, progress to tying each other to the bedstead with something soft and unthreatening like a silk scarf or feather boa. If this becomes a regular part of your bedroom routine, why not invest in some professional restraints? See pages 153–55 for ideas.

Use your power to tease your partner physically: this isn't about inflicting pain on your lover, but about reinforcing the fact that he or she is utterly

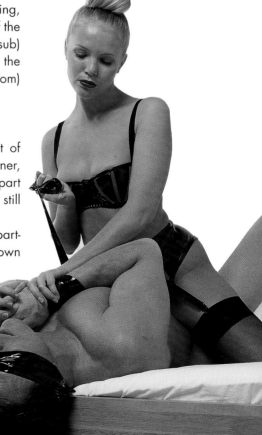

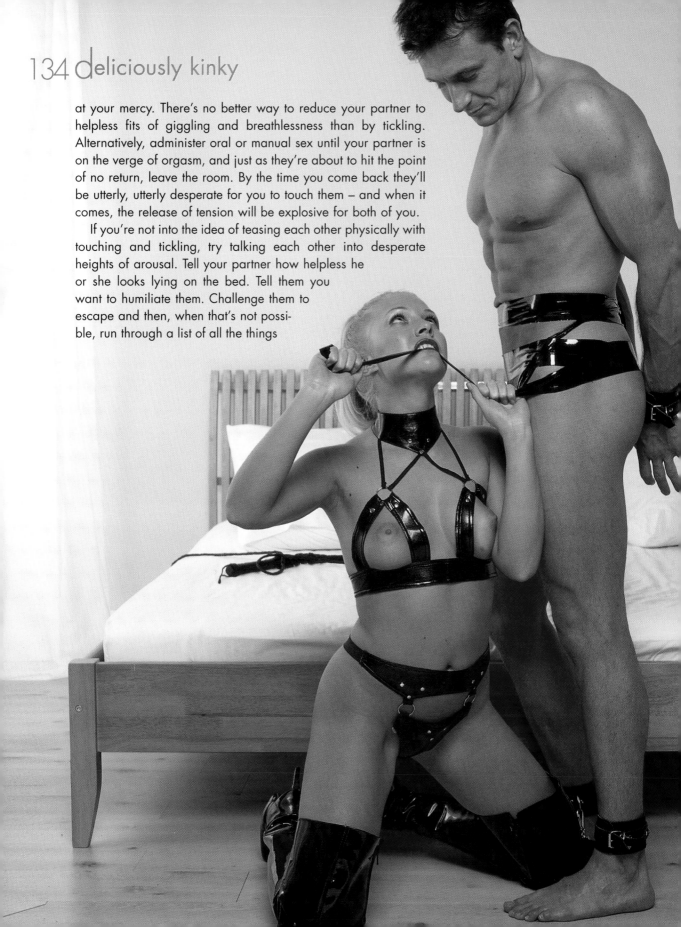

at your mercy. There's no better way to reduce your partner to helpless fits of giggling and breathlessness than by tickling. Alternatively, administer oral or manual sex until your partner is on the verge of orgasm, and just as they're about to hit the point of no return, leave the room. By the time you come back they'll be utterly, utterly desperate for you to touch them – and when it comes, the release of tension will be explosive for both of you.

If you're not into the idea of teasing each other physically with touching and tickling, try talking each other into desperate heights of arousal. Tell your partner how helpless he or she looks lying on the bed. Tell them you want to humiliate them. Challenge them to escape and then, when that's not possible, run through a list of all the things you'd like to do to them. Crack a whip on the floor as you speak to drive your point home. Speak as though you're just wondering aloud – don't look at your partner.

Like alcohol, or anything else you use to get a kind of high, sex games can become 'habituating'. This means you may find you need more and more each time to hit the high, and your behaviour and practices can become more and more extreme. If you're worried that your sex life is taking a turn for the sinister, go back to straight love-making for a few weeks.

Dos and don'ts

Bondage is only fun if you trust each other. Like all games, this one has rules – and these are totally unbreakable.

● DO agree on what you will and won't do before you start. It's important that you both have the same idea of how far is too far.

● DON'T enter into any bondage games under the influence of alcohol, drugs or any other mood-altering substances. Your judgement is impaired both mentally and physically and you may find yourself entering into a game that's out of your depth, or administering or receiving more pain than you could otherwise take.

● DO make sure you're with a partner you know and trust. The usual dating rules still apply.

● DON'T conceal health issues of any kind. For example, if you're asthmatic, don't play games that restrict your breathing. If you have back injuries, don't clamber onto a stretching rack.

● DO have a safe word that means 'stop'. Because you'll be playing games where 'no' means 'yes', you need a neutral word, like 'butterfly' or 'curtain', that has no sexual connotation. On hearing this word, you *must* release your partner from any restraining equipment and stop the game.

● DON'T use restraints like nipple clamps until you've tried them on yourself first. How else will you know how much is enough?

● DO end the session with a nice long hug and tender words, just as you would after straight sex. Emotions will be running high and this will help you both 'come down' from the adrenaline rush.

● DON'T let bondage get in the way of safe sex: use black or ribbed condoms if it helps contribute to the atmosphere.

● DO be honest – if the game stops being sexy, or you feel faint or nauseous, or you're frightened, bail out. Don't be scared to use your safe word.

● DON'T leave people alone for more than a minute at a time. It's part of bondage play to pretend to abandon your lover, but this can be dangerous. Never leave someone tied up, even for a moment, if they're wearing a mask, a gag or anything that restricts breathing.

SM and erotic pain

SM role-play

Reinforce the roles in your power relationships with these kinky games:

● If you're out in public, the dom should insist the sub asks his or her permission before using the bathroom.

● The dom leads the sub around the house in a collar and lead.

● The dom handcuffs the sub to the stairs, just out of reach of something the sub loves – whether it's a glass of wine or a cigarette.

● The sub refers to the dom as 'master' or 'mistress' at all times and doesn't speak unless spoken to, unless it's to say 'How may I best serve you?'

● Make a 'cage' for the slave, even if it's just shutting him or her in the wardrobe for half an hour. Keep watch on the sub, taunting and teasing from where you stand guard.

● The sub should offer to carry the dom's bags at all times.

Bondage is basically about power, not pain, but a lot of couples find that giving or receiving physical 'punishment' really enhances their tying-up games. This 'punishment' can range from the very mild and teasing to the more hardcore, inflicting slaps or strokes with a custom-made whip or paddle.

Everyone who enjoys erotic pain has his or her own theory as to why it's fun. Some people who climax through pain alone think of it as 'extreme stimulation'. Sometimes the pain satisfies a psychological need rather than a physical one: submissives get off not on the sensation itself but on the feeling of utter surrender. Pain mimics the signs of sexual arousal – it gets blood rushing to the surface of the skin and makes us cry out. It's also a fact that the more aroused we get, the more pain we're able to take – the hormones that flow through our bloodstream when we're at the excitement level of sexual arousal act as anaesthetics.

Sex games that involve inflicting pain are referred to as SM, which stands for sadomasochism. The dominant takes the role of the 'sadist', a term describing a person who gets a buzz out of wielding power and inflicting pain on his or her partner. The submissive takes on the role of the masochist – someone who obtains sexual gratification from receiving pain. Sometimes the pain is dished out as a 'punishment' during master–slave games. For example, a sub who forgets to obey one of the rules of the game, or doesn't show enough respect to his or her master, can expect a spanking or whipping to teach him or her a lesson. The pain can also be administered as a reward – a thank you, perhaps, for performing oral sex.

As ever, start at the soft end and increase to a level with which you're both happy. To begin with, don't use any toys – use your hands to slap, pinch and tickle each other. Find out what kind of touch you like: if you prefer the sharp sting of a slap, you'll enjoy

whips. If you relish the feeling of a blow to your body, invest in a paddle. If you like to be pinched, you'll love nipple clamps. No self-respecting SM couple's home is complete without a dungeon – this can be a room set aside for games, a wardrobe stuffed with leather gear and whips and chains, or a simple box under the bed that holds your favourite toys.

The dos and don'ts of bondage apply to SM play too. If you're new to giving or receiving pain, don't experiment with bondage at the same time. Learn your personal threshold for both types of games before you think of combining the two – it's easy to get overwhelmed and out of your depth. If at any point you become frightened or the pain stops being enjoyable, use your safe word and *stop*.

Top 10 fetishes

1 Shoes and feet
2 Leather and rubber
3 SM and bondage
4 Piercing
5 Uniforms
6 Hats
7 Food
8 Semen
9 Urine
10 Tattoos

Fetishes

The word 'fetish' comes from a medieval Portuguese word, *fetich*, meaning a religious relic that's believed to have magical properties. The modern dictionary definition of the fetish is an item that's necessary for sexual arousal: in short, it's about getting turned on by a thing rather than a person. So the woman who's only in the mood for sex when her boyfriend's wearing a cowboy hat and holsters, or the man who can only achieve an erection when his partner's wearing thigh-high rubber boots: they're fetishists.

You name it, someone, somewhere fetishises it. The most common fetishes are listed on the left. A quick browse through an Internet search engine for your own fetish will soon reveal you're not alone. Fetishists often upset partners because it appears that the fetishised item is more important than the lover. If this is the case with you, make the effort to enjoy 'straight' sex sometimes, or do a deal with your lover. Promise that if he or she doesn't mind dressing up for you, you'll give them the back rub you know they love.

long-distance loving

Many of us today have long-distance relationships. While it's hard missing someone, and having to readjust to his or her company after separations, long-distance relationships have the potential to stay romantic and fresh for a long time. With these tried and trusted techniques, absence really will make the heart – not to mention other more interesting parts of your anatomy – grow fonder.

Phone sex

You may not be able to speak every day, so when you do, don't waste a word. Make love down the line with a bout of phone sex. Surprise your lover halfway through a normal conversation by saying 'Do you miss me? I miss you. Here's how much…' and then go on to describe what you're going to do to each other the next time you meet. Describe what you're wearing and how you're feeling. The success is in the details: from the colour of your underwear to the beads of sweat trickling down between your breasts. The beauty of phone sex is that you can be your partner's fantasy: fresh and sweaty from the gym the way you know he loves it, or decked out in stockings and suspenders even if you're actually sitting in your dressing gown in front of the television.

'I can feel your big, hard, dick thrusting inside me.'

To make it really thrilling, call from your desk at work, from a public phone box, or from your mobile in a busy restaurant. This is a fantasy, so close your eyes and imagine you really are having sex

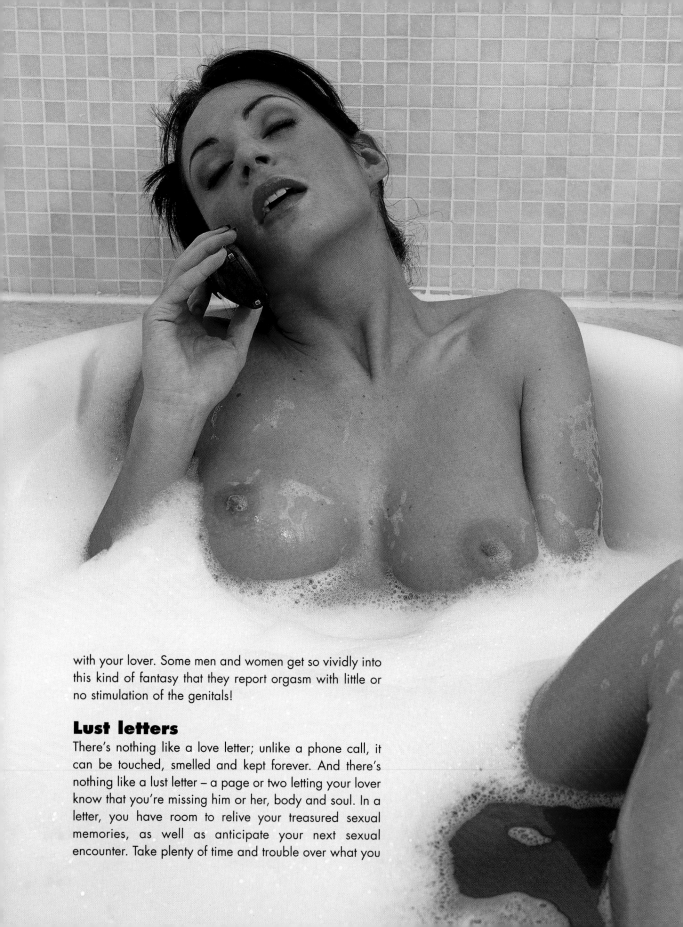

with your lover. Some men and women get so vividly into this kind of fantasy that they report orgasm with little or no stimulation of the genitals!

Lust letters

There's nothing like a love letter; unlike a phone call, it can be touched, smelled and kept forever. And there's nothing like a lust letter – a page or two letting your lover know that you're missing him or her, body and soul. In a letter, you have room to relive your treasured sexual memories, as well as anticipate your next sexual encounter. Take plenty of time and trouble over what you write, using quality, watermarked paper and a fountain pen. Hand write it even if you're not one of nature's calligraphers – this is the nearest thing your lover has got to you, and the more of your physical self you put into it the more it'll be worth. Draft it on a computer first if this helps. Scent the paper with your cologne or enclose a pair of panties you know your lover likes to remind him just what he's missing. If you're feeling super-sexy, wear them for a couple of hours first so that your own musky, natural scent impregnates them. Seal the envelope with a kiss.

Cybersex

Email flirting is the newest way of keeping in touch with a long-distance lover and combines the immediacy of a phone call with the permanence of a letter – print it out and keep it forever. It's fast and furious. The anonymity of the computer screen also means you can unleash your wild side. Words or fantasies you feel too self-conscious to say to someone who knows you well can come tumbling out in the frenzy of typing. The technologically minded among you may even want to get a webcam so you can watch each other type – and even put on a long-distance, private sex show for each other.

To really add spice, why don't you both go online in a sex chatroom and talk to each other as strangers? It's a great, safe way of indulging your fantasies. For example, if you both agree you find the idea of an orgy really sexy but don't actually want to do it, check out a swingers or group sex chatroom, log on and indulge, knowing you've got your partner there.

Cybersex needn't be confined to those in long-term relationships who don't see enough of each other: it's also a cheap, easy and safe way to get kicks for people who are single, or even for those in a relationship who simply need to let off a bit of steam without actually being unfaithful.

Cybersex has been a godsend for people who get off on anonymity – you never know exactly who you're talking to, and that's part of the thrill. When you log on to a chatroom, you have to give a name and a brief description, but it's not monitored so you can reinvent yourself and become the person of your fantasies.

Unlike conventional chatrooms, there's no real etiquette – the whole attraction of cybersex is that it's wild and anything goes. But as a very general rule, women want to be chatted up a bit first, while men barge in with explicit dialogue and tend to leave the chatroom as soon as they've, ahem, satisfied themselves. Some people do report, however, that after the 'climax' of their conversation, it's nice to hear an 'mmm' or a 'thank you' or a 'that was marvellous' rather than just stony silence.

9

Sexy playthings

the food of love

It's only natural that so many of us want to incorporate food and drink into our lovemaking: food and sex are two of life's main sensual pleasures. Food is part of the 21st-century mating ritual – it's traditional for us to wine and dine before we sixty-nine, and there's something very intimate about preparing and giving food to a lover. In fact, some evolutionists believe that kissing originates from primates feeding their young with food from their own mouths, an act as tender and loving as kissing itself. It's actually not a great idea to eat large amounts of rich food before sex – nothing kills the mood quicker than heavy bellies and indigestion. But it is worth feeding each other a few choice aphrodisiacs.

An aphrodisiac is any food or drink that ups the sex drive. Liquorice, fennel and ginger are proven aphrodisiacs, and any hot spicy food will cause blood to flow to the genitals and bring a flush to the cheeks, mimicking the advanced stages of sexual arousal in both sexes.

Turn yourselves into a dining-room table and eat your dinner off each other.

Some traditional aphrodisiacs earned their reputation for their taste and appearance as much as their nutritional content: oysters are wet and slippery, like the vagina, taste salty like semen, and have to be eaten with real gusto, with a pink tongue poking out to whip it down the throat. And then there's asparagus, a legendary aphrodisiac and a rather phallic-looking stalky vegetable.

Try eating food off each other: pasta isn't too hot and feels wonderfully slippery on naked skin. Play games where one of you hides a grape somewhere on the body and the other one has to guess where it is. Cover each other with chocolate body paint and lick it off. Write rude suggestions on each other's bodies, or slap on some chocolate paint in a well-hidden area and challenge your partner to lick you all over until he or she finds it. And it gets better: studies have shown that eating chocolate actually produces a hormone similar to phenylethylamine or PEA, a kind of endorphin secreted during sexual arousal.

Experiment with other foods, too. Honey, cream, exotic fruits and ice cream all make a deliciously sexy feast. You needn't stick to sweet foods, either: a cold, peeled cucumber lightly trailing along her labia or teasing the entrance to his anus is unlike anything either of you have ever felt before! And a recent study showed that the smell of cucumbers can actually raise testosterone levels in women.

Champagne not only tastes great but all those little bubbles popping against your skin is a sensual experience not to be missed (and one you can create with sparkling mineral water if you don't drink alcohol). Try having it in your mouths before oral sex, licking it off each other's nipples, his balls and her vagina. Alcohol can get you in the mood for sex and loosen your inhibitions, but have more than a glass or two and it won't help your sex life at all. You're more likely to have unprotected sex, to take dangerous risks and sleep with someone you wouldn't touch in the sober light of day. It can also give men brewer's droop (the inability to achieve erection) and can dehydrate women so it's hard for them to lubricate during sex.

amorous attire

Most of us tend to make love naked and, especially when we've been in a relationship for some time, give little thought to what we wear to the bedroom. But clothes can be a great way for us to express our sexuality without words, to tease our partner and bring an element of novelty back into the bedroom. There's something highly erotic and teasing about not being able to see the whole body, straight away. Men in particular say that the mere sight of their lover in exotic lingerie is enough to send them over the edge... Some people dress up simply as a prelude to making naked love, while others like to keep an item of clothing on throughout.

When choosing lingerie, the most important thing is that you're true to yourself. If you're not comfortable with the idea of basques, suspenders and fishnets, there are plenty of alternatives. Try a more exotic variation on the theme of your usual lingerie. If you're used to plain, sporty underwear, for example, look at the lingerie influenced by clubwear, which generally consists of simple, Lycra garments decorated with sequins and sparkles. Wear something in which you feel sexy and comfortable and you can be sure it'll be reflected in your sexual performance.

That said, it's only polite to take your partner's preferences into consideration. Look at the advertisements, films and images that arouse him and try to incorporate similar elements into your own sexy style. This goes for men, too – next time your lover lingers over a gorgeous male model in a particular brand of underwear in her glossy magazine, take note!

● Lace is sexy not only because of the teasing glimpse it gives of the skin on the other side, but also because it lightly tickles your body the whole time, preparing you for your lover's touch. If you like to wear your lingerie while you're making love but still want your most sensitive erogenous zones exposed, then crotchless panties and

Colour me sexy

The colour of your underwear can be as powerful as its style.

● Black suggests sophistication. It's also the colour of SM clothes, so it's not as safe as it seems. Be a queen of the night with a negligée or transparent dressing gown in black: not only is it classy, it's also slimming.

● Sometimes the sexiest underwear is simple white cotton – it's cool, comfortable, and there's something virginal about it. Wear white when you want to recapture the thrill of your first sexual experience.

● Silver or gold suggests special occasion sex and has a hint of sex industry worker about it – it's certainly not everyday lingerie. Put on the glitz when you want to give him a night to remember! Great if you're performing a striptease or lap dance.

● Just the mention of red lingerie is enough to turn grown men into gibbering teenagers. Traditionally worn by prostitutes, red speaks for itself, and says you're sexually confident, experienced and hungry.

nipple-slash bras are for you. This lacy lingerie gives both of you easy access to your nipples, clitoris and vaginal lips...but you never have to get undressed.

● If you're into fast sex, invest in a bra and panties set fastened with ribbons: one tug and you're naked. There's something very animalistic about your man literally ripping your underwear off you – especially if he does it with his teeth...

● Stockings versus tights: there is no debate! While nothing beats pantyhose for comfort, they're nigh on impossible to take off sexily. Stockings make legs look much longer, slimmer and more shapely; keep them on during sex, or use your stockinged feet to massage his back – and his front.

● Some of the most extreme lingerie available is influenced by bondage gear: it's impossible to forget you're wearing a leather bra with chain mail cups, and the matching panties will stimulate you long before you start touching each other. Wear them underneath your regular clothes all day to get you in the mood for the night ahead. The thought that your work colleagues and friends might hear the clanking of the chain mail underneath your work suit is part of the thrill.

● Underwear this sexy needn't be confined to the bedroom. Try wearing nothing else underneath a PVC trench coat, or a fur coat. Next time you pick your partner up from work, the pub, the train station, his five-a-side football match, anywhere – teasingly flash him from the car. It will drive him wild to know his friends are so near his sexy woman...but that you're going home with him.

● Oh and ladies, one final word on lingerie. Sometimes it's really true that less is more. Go out without *any* lingerie on at all, whisper to your man in a packed place that you're not wearing any knickers and watch as his jaw hits the floor.

Feathers and other fabrics

When we're dressing for sex, touch is as important as sight – we instinctively go for unusual, tactile materials like silks, feathers and rubber to enhance our sensual experience.

Rubber So it takes a little longer to squeeze into rubber trousers than it does to slip on a pair of jeans, but rubber-lovers the world over agree it's worth the extra effort. The softer rubber that's used to imitate leather feels as natural as a lover's caress, but it's the full-on fake stuff that has the real cult following, with a huge range of underwear and outerwear available. Many devotees say the sticky, restrictive feel of rubber against the skin alone speeds up their orgasm, and a few even report becoming aroused at the smell of the talcum powder that you need to use to get the rubber garments on! Rubber isn't a breathable fibre like cotton, so it makes you sweat, releasing pheromones – your natural, highly aphrodisiac animal scent. If you fancy yourself as a budding fashion designer, it's easy to make your own rubber clothes with liquid latex, which shrinks deliciously as it dries against the body. Or mummify yourself with bodywrap tape, which also makes a great blindfold or wrist restraint.

Silk Sexy and classy, silk is the most romantic of fabrics and needn't be confined to your clothes – cover your bed in silk sheets and be amazed at how sensuous your lovemaking becomes. It has the added benefit of being a natural fibre which lets the skin breathe. It doesn't come cheap, but the luxury aspect of silk will only enhance your enjoyment of it. Dress yourself in silk from the skin up and feel sexy throughout the day, no matter what else you're wearing.

Save red underwear for those sexy days when you feel like a scarlet woman.

Feathers Fabulous for lovers who tease to please! Tickling is the best, safest way to experience that fine line between pleasure and pain, and we have yet to invent a tickle stick as effective as the humble feather! For a touch of Moulin Rouge decadence, incorporate marabou slippers and feather-trimmed lingerie into your lovemaking, or, if you usually tie each other up with handcuffs, try restraining each other with a feather boa tied tightly around the wrists. Trace feathers on each other's inner thighs, eyelids, lips and anywhere else your skin is thin and sensitive. Go really wild with huge peacock or ostrich feathers that you can use to lightly slap each other. And, if the mood takes you, turn a feather into a quill and use it to write steamy suggestions on a piece of paper.

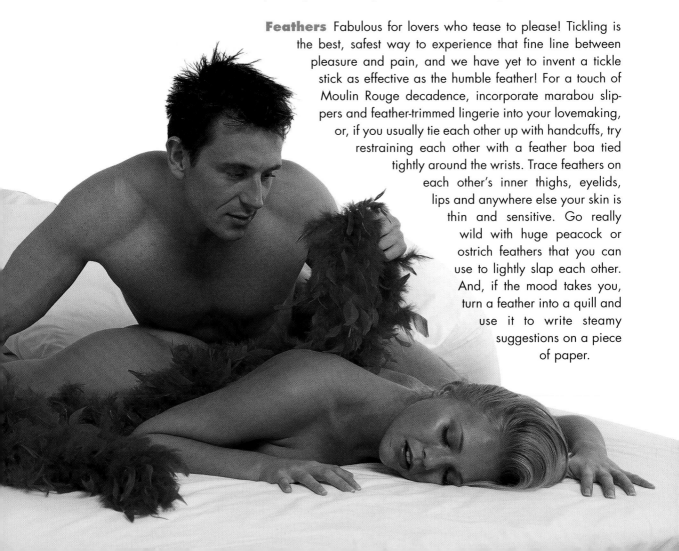

Sexy accessories

Whoever said that diamonds were a girl's best friend obviously didn't have a vibrator: sexy playthings enhance your lovemaking and give you a new, erotic lease of lust whether you're with a partner or flying solo.

Oils, lotions and potions

These help the course of true love run even smoother. If you think you don't need a lubricant, think again! Lubricants fall into two categories: water-based and oil-based ones.

Water-based lubricants are safe to use in places where the sun never shines as, used properly, they're highly unlikely to cause an allergic reaction or an infection, and are condom-friendly. For intercourse, look for a long-lasting, colourless, odourless brand that's the nearest thing you can get to the body's natural moisture (and won't stain the sheets). Water-based lubes are also safe to use with sex toys (which should never be used internally without a lubricant); some of the newer vibrators and dildos are made of silicone and can be broken down by oil.

Oil-based products make great massage oils. You can also have fabulous slippery, sliding sex by rubbing the oil into one another's chests and then making love in the missionary position. To really wake your skin up, most sex shops stock special heat-activated massage oil, which warms up when you blow on it or lick it, or minty gels that tingle invigoratingly as they're massaged into the skin. And there's more good news for those of you with a sweet tooth: flavoured massage oils can be used during oral sex (or if you prefer, diluted fruit juice), which are guaranteed to turn him into your boy lollipop!

Seductively massage some lubricant all over your body before you start to make love.

A word of warning, though: if you're using condoms, always check the label of your lubricant before applying it. If you see the word 'oil' anywhere in the small print, don't use it. Oil can rot latex, and you won't be having safe sex.

Sight and sound

Mirror, mirror, on the ceiling, what's that lovely sexy feeling? If you've never made love in front of your own reflection, you don't know what you're missing. Mirrors are a great way to enhance rear-entry sex – a lot of women say they love the sensation in this position but miss the eye contact. Mirrors take care of that. And if you're bored of your favourite old sex position, watching yourself can give you a whole new appetite for it. Mirrors give you the chance to see your lovemaking from an entirely new angle – great if the sight of a penis sliding in and out of a vagina turns you on. If you can't hang a mirror from the ceiling, or you feel self-conscious about your body, place a mirror over a mantelpiece and watch your faces as you enjoy rear-entry sex standing up against the fireplace. Or, for some sexy foreplay, have your partner shave your pubic hair while you watch in a hand-held mirror.

At the other end of the scale, you could invest in a blindfold – the sexy alternative to sex with the lights out. We rely on visual stimulation for arousal, but when sight is taken away, every other sense becomes much more responsive. Blindfolds are available in luxurious padded leather or PVC so you can mix and match them with the rest of your fetish wardrobe. The element of helplessness and domination – depending on which of you is wearing the blindfold – can be hugely arousing, too. Surprise the blindfolded lover with kisses in strange places!

And, if you've been following all the sex tips in this book, you might need to buy a ball gag – after all, you don't want your screams of pleasure to wake up the whole neighbourhood!

Dildos and vibrators

Sex is one of the few areas of life in which adults are allowed to play, to return to the simple sensual pleasures. And what would play-time be without a toy box full of dildos, vibrators and all the other adult playthings to enhance and enrich your sex life?

Sex toys are nothing new. People have been using fake penises to get themselves off since stone-age woman first found a novel use for that interestingly shaped piece of flint (and there are cave paintings to prove this). Happily, the 21st-century girl has more options. Modern sex toys are made of anything from leather to rubber, plastic or silicone. Some are the size and shape of a small lipstick and slip discreetly in your handbag – others are twelve inches long and appear to have motors that could power a small motorbike. Dildos are moulded in the shape of penises and designed for internal use while vibrators are battery-powered toys that are intended mainly for clitoral massage and stimulation. Some very clever toys manage to do both at once. Whatever your sexual style, status and situation, there's a sex toy that's right for you.

Vibrators have traditionally been associated with self-pleasure, and not without reason. Many a woman has turned to her faithful friend in her bedside drawer when she hasn't had a relationship for a while, when her lover is away or when she just wants a quick, easy climax. But while vibrators and dildos are a great way to enhance solo sex, these toys aren't just for singles. More and more couples are finding that introducing sex aids to their lovemaking brings greater intimacy, more orgasms and a whole new sense of fun to the bedroom. In fact, certain sex toys were designed specifically for use during intercourse – the latest product is a marriage between the traditionally male cock ring and the female vibrator.

Strap-on dildos are popular with lesbians who enjoy feeling something inside them – leather ones are particularly popular because of their realistic feel. Double-ended dildos are great for lesbian lovers who want to enjoy simultaneous penetration – sitting opposite each other gives them great access to one another's clitorises. Double penetration dildos have an attachment for the anus as well as the vagina.

Pleasure balls

This peculiar-looking device for the woman consists of two balls connected by a cord: each ball contains ball bearings that move around inside the outer spheres, creating subtle sensations. Placed in the vagina, they're great for toning pelvic floor muscles as these muscles are used to hold the balls in place. And stronger PC muscles make for better, stronger orgasms. What's more, inserting and gently pulling the cord on the balls while masturbating can cause fantastic internal sensations. Some women report walking around on the brink of orgasm for hours, others say it feels similar to having a penis inside. Make sure you use lube, and don't insert them into the rectum. It's not a good idea to use love balls during intercourse, but if you want to include your lover and introduce him to your love balls, ask him to put them inside you or take them out.

Toys for boys

These fall into two camps: first, there are penis rings, also known as cock rings or Arab straps. These are designed to be slipped over the balls and penis before it's completely erect: once the penis is fully erect, the blood is trapped, which means the erection will last for much longer than it otherwise would. Penis rings are available in metal (and come in a range of sizes) or slightly stretchier rubber: first-timers should use rubber, as it's more flexible.

Second, there are anal plugs, also available in different sizes, and vibrators, designed to stimulate the male G-spot, which is a few centimetres or so up the anus (see page 11). Many men like to use anal toys in conjunction with masturbation or oral sex rather than intercourse. Unlike vaginal dildos, anal toys often have a handle to stop them vanishing all the way up. They can be pulled out of the anus as climax approaches to enhance orgasm. All anal toys should be used with a good lubricant as this part of the body doesn't produce its own natural moisture – and of course hygiene is all-important here.

Restraints, whips and paddles

No bondage aficionado's bedroom is complete without a home dungeon, and there are a few basics you can't be without. Most people who are into restraint during sex start with handcuffs. Try the fur-lined ones first – they're fun and unintimidating. The more solid, tougher metal ones are more uncomfortable, which is part of the appeal for many people. Just as restrictive but more wearable are the leather ones, which coordinate better with other SM accessories. Also available in

black leather, leg irons or 'spreader bars' keep your legs apart, leaving the genitals helplessly exposed. To complete the look, go for a full-body harness, which has special loops and clips for the handcuffs and leg irons.

Whips are surprisingly versatile and can be used for so much more than whipping. If pain doesn't turn you on, try trailing a leather whip over each other's erogenous zones, or loosely wrapping it around each other's wrists to create a gentle restraint. If a little bit of pain does do it for you, gently experiment with the multi-lashed cat-o'-nine-tails, which delivers lots of little stinging sensations at once rather than concentrating the blow in one place. It makes sense to whip the tougher parts of the body, like thighs, backs and legs. Be very, very careful if you're using a whip on nipples and genitalia. They're much more delicate than you might think!

You can use the back of your hand or the back of a hairbrush for playing spanking games, but custom-made paddles are safer and sexier. Here comes the science bit: spanking increases blood flow to the genitals and flushes the skin, mimicking the body's signs of extreme arousal, so it actually speeds you on your journey towards orgasm. If you're going to spank, make sure you stick to the fleshier areas of the body like the buttocks and thighs. Avoid the lower back, because that's where the kidneys are and you could damage yourself even if you don't realise it: when you're turned on, the endorphins released (the pleasure hormones that rush around your body during sex, driving you wild) can actually dull your ability to feel pain, allowing you to get carried away.

Collars and leads

Studded leather and PVC chokers have become mainstream fashion items, but few people who wear them know their kinky history. 'Collaring' is an SM term that refers to the act of 'enslaving' your partner. Some of the furry collars designed for private use wouldn't look out of place in a regular club, and many SM couples wear more subtle chokers when they're out and about in everyday life – only those in the know will recognise the symbolism.

Attach a lead to the collar and parade your lover around the house: during intercourse, use the collar and lead to guide your partner into the position of your choice, much as you'd use the lead to 'steer' your dog when you're walking him. If you're playing games where you order your partner about, it can be fun to use terms like 'sit' and 'walkies' – and the lead is a great restraint if you want to jerk your partner's neck gently during doggy-style sex. You can also pull gently on a collar during oral sex to indicate what you want your partner to do to you.

erotica and porn

Pornography refers to graphic, explicit depictions of any sexual act – whether that's between a man and a woman, two men, two women, one man and two women, one woman and four men... you get the picture. According to conventional wisdom, only men get off on watching porn because they are more visually aroused than women; this is becoming less true every day.

Pornography is most often enjoyed alone, but it is increasingly being used by couples who want to enhance their sex lives. If you're going to watch porn with a lover, the most important thing is to find a theme you both agree on: with a huge range of genres available – from straight sex, same sex and group sex, to totally shaven actors, and actresses with huge breasts, to name but a few – there's bound to be something that tickles both your fancies. It can be a matter of minutes

Watched together, porn can be a great way to find out about each other's fantasies.

from remarking that what the couple on screen are doing looks sexy to moving to the bedroom upstairs and re-enacting it yourselves. But with so many hundreds of thousands of products out there, how do you choose the right one for you? Here's a guide to four of the most popular media.

The internet Surfing around for websites that turn you on can be great fun with a partner. It's discreet, private (assuming you're accessing the internet on your home PC and not at work), new and exciting, but internet porn isn't without its downsides. For a start, it can get expensive (most sites require a credit card before you can access them), pictures can be annoyingly small, and some take so long to download you lose the incentive to be aroused. Because the internet is uncensored, there's also the danger of stumbling across distasteful or illegal images.

Erotica and novels Erotica tends to be more literary and artistic than porn, and as a result is hugely popular with women. Erotic novels are usually packed with thrillingly explicit sexual content in the context of a well-written story. They often have a specific theme, for example, lesbian interest, slave games or even sci-fi and adventure. Because reading is such an intimate, interactive activity, these books are great enjoyed alone. The only drawback is that it is quite tricky to hold the book open, turn the pages and masturbate at the same time. You can overcome this problem by using a vibrator that straps to your clitoris, or, if you're not alone, getting someone to read aloud to you, or to masturbate you, go down on you, or hold a vibrator against you while you read.

Magazines These are easy to come by and relatively cheap. Most young boys get their first taste for pornography through magazines, which explains why many of them hold these publications so dear; but many women are into them, too. Magazines can be taken anywhere, and generally combine words and pictures, with arousing stories or interviews to go with the images. They're often quite specialised and will have adverts and contact numbers for other publications and films along the same lines. The fact that you can easily prop a magazine between your legs, on a bed or table top, and have both hands free for whatever takes your fancy is also an undeniable advantage.

Movies These are widely available, inexpensive and a great way to pass the time when there's nothing decent on the television! Movies are a nice, passive type of pornography, requiring little interaction. They are also a great way to enjoy pornography with your partner: you can talk over it, copy the action or just collapse on the sofa and wait for it to work its magic. Once the film is running, no interaction is required; you can just sit there and enjoy. Some viewers complain that it doesn't take long to get bored of a film, but many adult shops run exchange schemes and there's never a shortage of new movies. And, with the advent of DVD technology, it's easier than ever to skip to the sexy parts!

index

Siobhan Kelly is Contributing Editor for *Cosmopolitan* magazine. She has written extensively on sex and relationships and has contributed to *Company, More!, Essentials, Cosmo Girl, heat* and *Sky* magazines.